Nutley Notables

The men and women who made a
memorable impact on our home town,
Nutley, New Jersey
Volume Two

ANTHONY BUCCINO

Nutley Notables:

The men and women who made a memorable impact
on our home town, Nutley, New Jersey

Volume Two

By Anthony Buccino

Published by
Cherry Blossom Press
PO Box 110252
NUTLEY NJ 07110

ISBN-10: 1728689481

ISBN-13: 978-1728689487

V 1.4

ACKNOWLEGEMENTS

Nutley Historical Society
Nutley Public Library and Staff
Nutley Hall of Fame
Mattia Awards
Nutley Yesterday-Today

Nutley Women's History Month Committee, March 2002
Women's History Panel, March 2014
Joanne Cocchiola, Rev. Jill Fenske, Eileen Poiani, Rosalie C.
Scheckel, Catherine Thorpe, Nancy Greulich, Phyllis Coldabella

Nutley Public Library Centennial Committee

Ann Troy, Vicky Chalk, Ronn Merritt, Phil White, Michael Gabriele,
Anthony Iannarone, Barry Lenson, Michael Perrone, Mary Ann
Fitton, Jeanetta LoCurio Brancaccio, Jeff Grieco, Lou Mascitello

Nutley Sun; Helen Maguire; Hasime Kukaj; Meghan Grant; Josh
Jongsma
TapIntoNutley; John Lee
Patch; Eric Kiefer
The Jersey Tomato; Diane Lilli

CONTENTS

1   **Notable Nutley Women**   5

2   **Artists, Musicians, Writers**   52

3   **Public Service**   67

4   **Business Leaders**   81

5   **Sports**   94

6   **Index**   112

7   **Nutley Notables, Vol. 1**   114

8   **Bibliography**   131

NOTABLE NUTLEY WOMEN

Beatrice Perry

In a small room, described as a shack, at 104 Passaic Avenue, Mrs. Beatrice Perry started the Rheinheimer Boys Club to provide recreational activities on a year round basis to boys. Perry worked for the organization for 24 years and was honored by a number of organizations, including Lions Club, as "Outstanding Nutley Citizen of the Year" in 1947.

"Originally called the "Croquet Club", the organization was later named for the late Mayor Walter Rheinheimer, one of the earliest supporters. Although founded as a club for Negro boys, it now has two white boys among its 15 members."

The organization was founded July 8, 1933. Mrs. Perry and her late husband William formed the club, and went to the then-Mayor Walter Rheinheimer to ask him for the use of town vehicles to transport the boys up to Schooley Mountain for a camping vacation. Rheinheimer was so impressed with her efforts that he went to the Rotary Club and Mrs. Perry was given the loan of 12 trucks. The mayor, himself, drove her and the oldest boys to the mountain in his car. His continued efforts with the club caused the boys to vote, after his death, that the club be named in his honor.

Sources: The Nutley Women's History Month Committee, March 2002; Notable Nutley Women, Women's History Panel, March 2014; Nutley Sun; Passaic Herald.

Gertrude Guenzler

In an undated photocopy of a feature story in the *Nutley Sun*, Gertrude Guenzler recalls pioneer life in our town, recalling Emily Avenue in 1900. "I came to Nutley when I was five, and we moved into one of the Ten Commandments," Mrs. Guenzler remembered.

The "Ten Commandments" is a row of ten houses located on Bloomfield Avenue across from Nichols Park. Guenzler, whose family name was Zitzmann, explained that they lived in the "eighth" commandment, "We lived down the street from the paper mill, which is now the "Park Pub."

At about 4:30 p.m., the women gathered in the park, pails flung over their arms, to get water for drinking and cooking: from the pump.

"The ten houses were really built to accommodate the people who worked at the hat shop factory," Guenzler noted. The building today is better known as the former Black Prince Distillery. [The Nichols Hat factory at what is now 800 Bloomfield Avenue later became the distillery which later was converted to offices, condos and at one time, the Eighth Floor Restaurant, on the first floor. It is owned by Roche in 2018.]

Where Hoffman-La Roche now stands, Guenzler recalls a huge woods where she and her sister, Carolyn, would romp, collecting hazel nuts, mushrooms, and peaches. The Klingers owned an orchard just beyond the Roche property, which is now Route 3.

The Nutley senior, who commented that people often mistake her for being younger because she has "dark hair and most of my teeth" remembers attending Yantacaw School and the sewing school for children.

"Don't you know, dear, that all the girls would go to these sewing classes, which were held upstairs in the Town Hall," she said. "We used to make long flannel petticoats."

When Guenzler was 16, she went to work at George La Monte's Paperwork Co. [The building, on the north side of the rail tracks from the hat factory, was part of Roche, but was demolished when the pharmaceutical giant moved to California.] Along with other employees of the time, she worked 12 hours a day and received $6 a week for her efforts.

"All the women had to wear dresses that met the top of their shoes," Guenzler said. "And every one of them had grosgrain ribbons in their hair."

"At Thanksgiving time, the employees of George La Monte would be a real spectacle as they paraded down the streets with their turkeys." The turkeys were courtesy of resident Tom O'Neill.

Sources: Nutley Sun by Mary Dominski; Nutley Celebrates Women. The Nutley Women's History Month Committee, March 2002; Notable Nutley Women, Women's History Panel, March 2014.

Elizabeth Stow Brown

In March 1907, Elizabeth Stow Brown compiled "The History of Nutley, Essex County, New Jersey." Ms. Stow Brown was involved in numerous civic organizations including the New Jersey Historical Society and the Nutley Women's Public School Auxiliary. The publication is a widely used source of information on the history of Nutley.

Sources: The Nutley Women's History Month Committee, March 2002; Notable Nutley Women, Women's History Panel, March 2014.

Jeanette M. Clendinning

The preschool she founded more than 70 years ago still bears her family name. But what few know is the story of the gumption Jeanette Clendinning rallied to fight Town Hall.

In July 1944, Clendinning of 126 High Street received a summons to appear before Town Recorder Edwin J. C. Joerg to answer a charge that her nursery school is operating in violation of Residence A restrictions, Town Attorney William Gorman gave a second opinion allowing the placement by the Social Service bureau, of eleven children in foster homes located in Residence A zones.

Health Officer Richard Fellers had earlier refused to license the eleven prospective foster homes based on the Town Attorney's first ruling that boarding homes are not permitted in Residence A zones.

The Town Attorney said that his opinion rendered in the Clendinning case does not necessarily affect the smaller boarding home for children where only one or two children are incidentally kept as part of a family unit.

Reversing a $50 fine inflicted by Recorder Edwin J.C. Joerg, a jury in Judge Naughright's Court of Common Pleas in Newark on Sept. 28, 1945, found Mrs. Robert W. Clendinning not guilty of having violated Nutley's zoning ordinance by conducting a nursery school at her home, 126 High Street.

Jeanette Clendinning fought the town for more than a year to keep open her nursery school despite the town building inspector's order.

The latest ruling should solve the problem posted by Mrs. Clendinning's custody of Judy Udal, daughter of Mr. and Mrs. William E. U. Udal now in England, whose nearest relative here, her grandfather, Burton S. Brown, died this week in Glen Falls, N.Y.

Decision in the case turned on the word "school" in Section 12 of the town's zoning ordinance governing activities in A residential zones. Admitting that Mrs. Clendinning's classes were a nursery school, Gorman argued that the framers of the ordinances, in using the word "school" meant a public school and not classes conducted for profit.

Mrs. Clendinning's counsel, John F. Leonard of Newark, contended that the word spoke for itself and that the Mrs. Clendening's group came within the meaning of the ordinance which make the operation of schools in A residential zones permissible.

The trial was marked by a mass of testimony which was not permitted by Recorder Joerg when he sustained objections by the town attorney at the original trial of the case in Nutley, August 4, 1944. At that time Mrs. Clendinning's counsel sought to have an array of witnesses testify to the educational nature of Mrs. Clendinning's activities. Judge Naughright allowed the testimony.

Jeanette Clendinning fought the law, Mrs. Clendinning won.

In October 1944, Jeanette and Robert Clendinning learned their son 1st Lt. Robert Clendinning Jr., of the Army Air Force, was reported killed in action Sept. 27 over England.

Sources: Nutley Sun, September 28, 1945, August 3, 1945, July 21, 1944. Oct. 20, 1944.

Nelle M. Anderson

Nelle M. Anderson was born in Indiana and lived in Nutley for a long time. Before she lived in Nutley, she was an active Suffragist, marching in parades and actively working for women's right to vote. She served as a secretary to the movement.

She had been greatly influenced by a Sunday school teacher at the Methodist church she attended in Indiana. There she learned that there was nothing evil about diversity, and that all human beings were endowed with the same emotions of hope aspiration, love, anxiety and fear.

Anderson brought her experiences with her when she moved here. She was instrumental in founding the Human Relations Council of Nutley on Nov. 21, 1950, due to the efforts of Nelle Anderson. The organization's goals included, fostering inter-group relations, and community outreach.

Many important programs were presented by this group including raising funds for a Rutgers scholarship in a workshop in human relations, educational audio-visual aids workshops and an audit to accumulate information on how to present information to the community on the status of human rights, a youth conference, and brotherhood week.

During brotherhood week in 1964, a ceremony honoring Anderson and celebrating her 80th birthday was held at the Nutley Museum. A review of the highlights of her life was read by one of her two sons, and a citation listing her accomplishments was read, followed by a presentation of flowers and mementos. The Nelle Andersen Scholarship Fund in Human Relations was created for Rutgers students, and friends contributed to it that evening.

Sources: Nutley Sun – Victoria Chalk; The Nutley Women's History Month Committee, March 2002; Notable Nutley Women, Women's History Panel, March 2014.

Elvira Kinsley

In 1904, Mrs. Elvira Kinsley invited a group of women to meet at her home on Prospect Street to form a Women's Club. This was the start of the first club for women in Nutley.

The Friday Afternoon Club, the oldest women's organization in town, whose object is to supply mutual help and improvement in the study of literature, art and general information, began in February 1904, when the late Mrs. [Elvira] William J. Kinsley, well-known or her interest in civic affairs invited a group of women to meet at Sunny Crest, her home on Prospect Street, with the idea of forming a club. Thus was organized the first club for women in Nutley, with Kinsley as president.

The founders of many other prominent organizations for women in Nutley came from this initial group, including the late Mrs. Perley Prior, the late Mrs. Joseph Little and Mrs. Horace Tantum, who were presidents of the Women's Club and the first three commissioners of the Girl Scout Council, Mrs. A.L. Harlan, the late Mrs. L.C. Pratt and Mrs. M.C.W Buchenberger.

During WWI the club contributed to a recreation hall for local soldiers and collected 550 books for them. The Nutley Library was started because of Mrs. Kingsley's efforts. She has been honored with the planting of a tree on the library lawn.

Sources: The Nutley Women's History Month Committee, March 2002; Notable Nutley Women, Women's History Panel, March 2014; Nutley Sun; NUTLEY Yesterday Today.

Dorinda Peddieson

Dorinda Catherine Crobaugh Peddieson was a well-known civic leader, serving as founding member of the Evening Department of the Nutley Women's Club. A 1972 recipient of the Dr. Virginius Mattia Award for outstanding community service, Peddieson served on the Nutley Board of Education for 18 years from 1954 to 1972. She also served on the advisory boards of the Nutley Adult School and the Nutley Health Department. Committed to being involved in community affairs, Peddieson volunteered at Clara Maass Medical Center, giving more than 11,000 hours. She served on the Vincent Methodist Church's Nutley Committee for Education and also chaired the Senior Awards Committee of the church.

Sources: The Nutley Women's History Month Committee, March 2002; Women's History Panel, March 2014, Mattia Awards.

Emma Jane Proal

Emma Jane Proal was the first president of the Nutley Women's Club. The Women's Club formally opened in 1912 with the one of the objectives to preserve the Vreeland House as a historical landmark.

Proal stated, "Guard well the democracy of this organization! Let it be the point of contact between the women of the township of Nutley as citizens, where class, creed, political differences, factions of all kinds may be laid aside and genuine desire for each other's good and the advancement of civic ideal for our town and state impel us toward united action."

Sources: The Nutley Women's History Month Committee, March 2002; Notable Nutley Women, Women's History Panel, March 2014.

Faith Walcott Morgan

Faith Walcott Morgan (April 7, 1869 to Dec. 19, 1964) may have made a larger impact on women's history after she left Nutley when she became a prominent suffragist in Virginia, but for the years she lived in town, she surely left her mark.

In 1914, the Women's Club of Nutley chose Morgan to be included in a "Founder's List" upon which clubs, on the payment of fifty dollars, may place in a beautifully bound and handsomely decorated volume, the names and accomplishments of some one woman they thus wish to specially honor for her general uplift work.

The club noted that Morgan for fifteen years was instrumental in maintaining the Nutley Sewing School, which started in with about fifty pupils, had subsequently as many as two hundred and fifty, and stopped only when Morgan was called away for family reasons to take up her residence in Hampton, Virginia.

Morgan was one of the group of women interested in the establishment of the Penny Provident Savings Fund in the Nutley public schools, and through all the years of her residence in the town was an earnest worker in the Nutley Improvement Society, most of the time holding the office of treasurer.

Finally, Morgan was a charter member of the Women's Club, leaving the town just at the beginning of its activities. These, however, were but a few only of Morgan's many public spirited activities during the years of her being a part of this community.

Her charities, numerous enough, were most unostentatious, but none the less worthy. She was sensitive to every appeal, extending help where it was most needed, from the pure kindness of her heart and her interest in humanity. When she left Nutley a void was created which has not been and cannot be easily filled.

Sources: Nutley Sun; Margaret Rhett, Encyclopedia Virginia (a partner of the Library of Virginia) History Panel, March 2014; Mattia Awards.

Lella Secor Florence

In 1917, Lella Faye Secor (1887-1966) married economist Philip Sargant Florence and they lived with their two sons at 115 Vreeland Avenue from 1919 to 1921, when they moved to Cambridge, England.

According to historian Geoffrey Batten, the house at that time was owned by Mary Sargant Florence who had lived there from 1889 to 1892, when Mary's husband drowned while swimming in Nichols Pond. When Lella and her family left for England in 1921, the house and land were sold separately.

In Cambridge, Lella became actively involved in campaigning for birth control, and for a period lived away from her husband in a flat in Paris. In 1929, Philip was appointed to the chair in commerce at the University of Birmingham and the couple moved to the Birmingham district of Selly Park, where they bought a large house called Highfield.

In 1930 she published Birth Control on Trial. Highfield became a focal point for the intellectual life of Birmingham in the 1930s – poet Louis MacNeice lived in the converted coachman's quarters and writer Walter Allen described how "Most English Left-Wing intellectuals and American intellectuals visiting Britain must have passed through Highfield between 1930 and 1950."

Lella remained committed to disarmament, birth control and women's rights and continued to write and campaign. She died of pneumonia following a stroke in 1966.

Sources: Geoffrey Batten, 2009; Wikipedia contributors. "Lella Secor Florence." Wikipedia, The Free Encyclopedia. Wikipedia, The Free Encyclopedia, 20 Apr. 2018. Web. 14 May. 2018.

Mary Sargant Florence

British painter Mary Sargant Florence (July 21, 1857 to Dec. 14, 1954) lived on Vreeland Avenue during the Nutley Artist and Writers Colony era from about 1888 to 1900.

She studied in Paris under Luc-Olivier Merson and at the Slade School under Alphonse Legros. She was a member of the New English Art Club and the Society of Painters in Tempera.

Florence was known for painting figure subjects, mural decorations in fresco and occasional landscapes in water color and pastel.

In 1888, she married Henry Smyth Florence, an American musician. They had two children: Philip Sargant Florence, the economist, and Alix Strachey, the psychoanalyst and translator of Freud.

Their home was demolished but the barn she converted into a studio has been converted into a private residence that still stands near the corner of Warren Street and Vreeland Avenue. Florence returned to England with her children after her husband Henry Smyth Florence drowned in Nichols Pond (or the Mud Hole) in 1892. She retained the studio until 1921.

Sources: The Nutley Women's History Month Committee, March 2002; Notable Nutley Women, Women's History Panel, March 2014; Cyndi Bostonian-Zacek; Mary Sargant Florence, https://en.wikipedia.org/w/index.php?title=Mary_Sargant_Florence&oldid=824114884 (last visited July 11, 2018).

Olive C. Sanford

Olive C. Sanford was born in Palmyra, N.Y., in 1875. She was graduated from Columbia University in 1898. She married Frederic Sanford in 1900, and for the next fifteen years lived in South America.

She was a resident of Nutley from 1915 to 1952. She devoted most of her life to improving public education and urging women to play a more important part in government and public affairs.

She served four terms as a member of the Nutley Board of Education from 1928 to 1934 and from 1937 to 1943.

She also served as president of the NJ State League of Women Voters. She was elected to the NJ State Legislature in 1934, continuing for eight terms as our Assemblywoman. During her years in Trenton, she campaigned for greater state support for public education, and attached the system of real estate taxes as the source of funding for education.

She was a strong advocate of progressive education and received an award for outstanding contribution to public education by the Essex County Education Association.

Sandford's last home in Nutley was "The Kingsley House" a rooming house at the corner of Nutley and Whitford avenues. She lived to age 95, spending her last years in the Valley Nursing Home in Westwood, NJ.

Sources: The Nutley Women's History Month Committee, March 2002; Notable Nutley Women, Women's History Panel, March.

Dorothea de St. Clement

Dorothea de St. Clement is the author of the books "White Gumbo" published in 1951 and "Prairies and Palaces" in 1963.

Mrs. de St. Clement was known here for her poem "I Love to Live in Nutley." According to Philip R. White, former editor of The Sun, Mrs. de St. Clement was asked to write the poem for the newspaper's 75th anniversary. Her poem is included in the Nutley Jaycees annual Distinguished Service Awards program.

She was the author of several books, the most well-known was "White Gumbo". "Prairies and Palaces" was collection of poems.

Born on March 7, 1888, in Chester, NJ, when she was five years old, her family moved Taylor, N.D., where they had the Taylor Hotel and later a sheep ranch outside of town. She attended the North Dakota Agricultural College at Fargo and taught in a prairie schoolhouse in Stark County, N.D.

Her literary talent blossomed as she contributed stories and poems to local newspapers and the children's page of magazines. While at college she wrote articles for farming papers on animal husbandry and stock raising.

She married Italian nobleman Count Giulio de Sauteiron de St. Clement of

Rome. A naturalized U.S. citizen, he worked with the Italian Steamship Lines in New York and Chicago. While living in Rome from 1921 to 1938, she wrote for stateside Italian newspapers including *La Tribuna D'Italia* and *The Italian Tribune*. She also wrote a syndicated column, "Travel Talk" while traveling the continent.

After the Count's death in 1935, she returned to the U.S. She lived at 30 Daily Place, Nutley, from 1954 until her death, at age 105, on June 24, 1984. In addition to her writing, she was a member of the Women's Club and the Animal Welfare League.

Sources: The Nutley Women's History Month Committee, March 2002; Notable Nutley Women, Women's History Panel, March 2014; Doreen LeBlanc.

Grace Seymour

Grace Seymour was the first woman to run for Nutley Board of Commissioners. In 1936, Seymour ran for the township governing board, and although unsuccessful, she announced in 1940 that she would make a second attempt. That effort resulted in her receiving 426 votes, finishing 14th in a field of 15 candidates.

Her published statement in 1940 read: "The last and not quite the least of these as an important factor, but believing that time logical to have a woman on the board. Not relegated to "Town Fathers" alone, but as a "Town Mother" to watch wait and serve the community. Wishing all running mates success, knowing if it is possible I should be elected that I can safely work with any four selected by the voters. I hereby thank them all for their courtesies to me, running alone/without organization, no manager and only my own small amount of money, without borrowing to pay expenses involved. The foregoing is not a horoscope and I have not been reading palms or the cards or tea leaves but a hardy expression of good faith."

In 2004, Joanne Cocchiola sought the commissioner seat vacated by her father, Frank after 28 years. As the first woman to be elected to the board, she garnered the most votes in the election and was named mayor.

Sources: The Nutley Women's History Month Committee, March 2002; Notable Nutley Women, Women's History Panel, March 2014.

Abbie Magee

Abbie Magee, a well-known political figure in Nutley, was the first woman in the state to be elected County Registrar of Deeds and Mortgages. Prior to that assignment, she was elected to the County Board of Freeholders and served on that committee from 1944 to 1950.

She was the first woman to serve as supervisor of the Bills in the State Legislature of New Jersey and was also Journal Clerk in the State Assembly. Magee was a charter member of the Tri Town Business and Professional Women's Club of Nutley, Bloomfield and Belleville.

She was active in political circles serving as the vice chairman of the Essex County Republican Party Committee for ten years. Magee was a delegate to the Republican National Convention in Chicago in 1952.

Sources: The Nutley Women's History Month Committee, March 2002; Notable Nutley Women, Women's History Panel, March 2014.

Ellen M. Berger

Born in Nutley in 1909, Ellen M. Berger attended NJ College for Women. She was a founder of the Nutley and Essex County Young Republicans. She was elected to the Assembly in 1954.

Sources: The Nutley Women's History Month Committee, March 2002; Notable Nutley Women, Women's History Panel, March 2014.

Dorothy Daggett Eldridge

Mayflower descendent Dorothy Daggett Eldridge had a great interest in civic affairs. She held the title of president of both the League of Women Voters and the American Association of University Women.

At the end of World War II she organized the Dumbarton Oaks Committee in Nutley to support the establishment of the United Nations. She founded and participated in numerous local and national civic organizations including the Nutley Human Relations Council, Martin Luther King Committee, Nutley Consumer Cooperative, Essex County Coalition for Human Priorities, Women's International League for Peace and Freedom, Nutley Democratic Club, and the American Civil Liberties Union.

Eldridge organized the New Jersey Chapter of SANE "Committee for a Safe Nuclear Policy," a national movement to control nuclear weapons testing, of which she ultimately was named its director.

The Nutley resident, a graduate of Mt. Holyoke College, was a microbiologist for Hoffman La Roche who resided here until her death in 1986. At the time of her death, Senator Frank Lautenberg and Senator Bill Bradley paid tribute to her life and efforts as an advocate of world peace.

Sources: Nutley Sun, Aug. 7, 1986; The Nutley Women's History Month Committee, March 2002; Notable Nutley Women, Women's History Panel, March 2014.

Dr. Elizabeth R. Brackett

Having started out as a Registered Nurse, Dr. Elizabeth Brackett received her M.D. from the College of Physicians and Surgeons of Columbia University. She opened her first office in Nutley in the 1930s where she started out as a pediatrician. She switched to a general practice and worked out of her home at 371 Franklin Avenue until 1960. She was on the medical staff of numerous hospitals.

In 1962, Dr. Brackett was selected as "woman of the year" by the New Jersey Branch of the American Women's Medical Association. She served as president of that chapter. She also served on the medical advisory board of the Visiting Nurse Association of Nutley.

Sources: Nutley Sun, March 8, 1962; The Nutley Women's History Month Committee, March 2002; Notable Nutley Women, Women's History Panel, March 2014.

Ada Weigel Powers

Ada Weigel Powers lived at 246 Grant Avenue in Nutley from 1910 to 1947. Born in Watertown, N.Y., in 1863, she graduated from Sherwood Academy of Music, Lyons, N.Y. For seventeen years she was concert pianist on the Pacific coast. She was the favorite accompanist for many well-known singers.

She was a composer of many songs; piano and violin compositions and known for her "leider", setting descriptive poems to music, such as Walt Whitman's "Invocation" and Tennyson's "Elaine". "Elaine" was first presented at Carnegie Hall by baritone David Bishpham, who later gave the work on tour. Many of her works were performed by the Nutley Symphony; in New York as well as elsewhere in the world.

Sources: The Nutley Women's History Month Committee, March 2002; Notable Nutley Women, Women's History Panel, March 2014.

Norma Hall

Norma Hall moved to Nutley in 1941 with her husband and daughter. Having formerly served as an air raid warden and on the Nutley Red Cross, she served on many committees and township boards. Hall founded the Community School in Nutley.

While serving as Religious Education Director of St. Paul's Congregational Church, she began to think about starting a town nursery school, as she felt there was a need for a non-profit nursery school that would provide the highest quality teaching at a reasonable cost. The Community School was started in 1967.

Sources: The Nutley Women's History Month Committee, March 2002; Notable Nutley Women, Women's History Panel, March 2014.

Anne Steele Marsh

Anne Steele Marsh (1901-1995) grew up in Nutley at 189 Walnut Street where her father, Frederic Dorr Steele, the illustrator of Sherlock Holmes, had his studio.

Growing up in such an artistic household with friends and neighbors also famous artists, it is no wonder she also became an artist of some reknown. Marsh studied art at Cooper Union in New York.

In 1925, she married a childhood friend, James Marsh, son of Frederick Dana Marsh, who lived and painted on The Enclosure. The couple lived in Greenwich Village before returning to New Jersey.

She had her first one-person show of paintings and wood engraving in 1934, and her work is in the permanent collection of the Metropolitan Museum, the Museum of Modern Art, the Philadelphia Museum of Art, the Library of Congress in Washington, D.C., the New Jersey State Museum in Trenton, as well as the Hunterdon Art Center.

The Marshes moved to Hunterdon County where they founded the Hunterdon Art Center in Clinton.

Sources: The Nutley Women's History Month Committee, March 2002; Notable Nutley Women, Women's History Panel, March 2014; Friends of the Hunterdon Art Center; Hunterdon Museum of Art.

Vivian Noyes Fikus

Vivian Noyes Fikus was one of Nutley's most well-known artists. A founding member of the Nutley Art Group, she served as its president for many years. She was the owner and operator of the Nutley Art Center at 200 Chestnut Street where she and fellow artists taught classes. She was a member of the Miniature Art Society of New Jersey.

Fikus designed Nutley's flag and seal. "The design's base is a field of gray upon which are superimposed three large acorns in red. Three wavy red lines beneath the acorns tie the design together and symbolize the location of Nutley on the Third River. The acorns are symbolic of the Town's name and its three centuries of history. In the center acorn, in white numerals, is the date, 1902, in which the year the town's name was changed from Franklin to Nutley.

"The town's ancient Indian, Dutch and English heritage is suggested on the first acorn. The middle acorn portrays one of the luxuriant nut trees for which Nutley was famous. A palette and quill pen with book refer to authors and writers who have lived here during the past century.

"The third acorn stresses the industrial life of the town. A sketch of the La Monte Paper Company plant with the numerals 1871 points out the date of the town's oldest active major industry. The electronic emblem indicates the Federal Telecommunications Laboratories while the caduceus refers to the Hoffmann-La Roche Company." [*Nutley Yesterday-Today*]

Under the name Vivian Noyes Fikus, she illustrated *Nutley Yesterday-Today* edited by Ann A. Troy and published by the Nutley Historical Society in 1961.

Born in Morristown, she lived in Nutley from 1946 until her death in 1981.

Sources: Nutley Celebrates Women. The Nutley Women's History Month Committee, March 2002; Notable Nutley Women, Women's History Panel, March 2014.

Louise Miller

Louise Miller served as vice chairman of the Nutley Red Cross for thirty-two years. She was a member of the original executive board. from the chapter's organization in 1917 until her death in 1959. She was recognized as a devoted and skilled leader and volunteer. A chapter resolution states "Her warmth of heart, her ability of character and her willingness to undertake any task, no matter how large or small makes her unique in the annals of Nutley and irreplaceable as an individual."

Sources: Nutley Yesterday-Today; Nutley Celebrates Women. The Nutley Women's History Month Committee, March 2002; Notable Nutley Women, Women's History Panel, March 2014.

Ruth N Keenan

Ruth N. Keenan, who designed and illustrated "Clara Maass: A Nurse, A Hospital", was a well-known Nutley commercial artist and portrait painter.

Her designs and illustrations were used by many northern New Jersey commercial firms and she painted a number of murals, including two in Clara Maass Memorial Hospital.

She also painted a series of lively storybook figures to decorate the pediatrics department of the hospital. Keenan's hand-painted trays were sold locally through at Filomena's Hobby Shop. Keenan published "Fire and Gold – an inspiring compendium of wisdom for living and loving" in 1973.

In 2002, using proceeds from the sale of her hand-painted trays, Keenan funded and instituted the Philomena Stefanelli Art Award at Nutley High School.

Born in 1911, Keenan lived at 6 Willow Place, and at age 92 began crafting and coloring her own greeting cards to market. She was also known locally for her many letters to the *Nutley Sun* editor.

Sources: Clara Maass: A Nurse, A Hospital, A Spirit; Fire and Gold; Mary Ann Fitton; Jeanetta LoCurio Brancaccio; Jeff Grieco.

Estelle Armstrong

Estelle Manon Armstrong, a noted artist and teacher, lived at 603 Bloomfield Avenue, Nutley, from 1922 until her death in 1977. The house is still standing, but the studio has been razed.

Her work, much of it in still life and flowers, is in the Rockefeller and other private collections as well as the universities of Oklahoma and West Virginia.

She won many awards, including the Eloise Egan Prize for her "White Iris" and a bronze medal from the American Beauty Society.

During the 1930s and early 1940s, Armstrong taught water color at New York University with her husband, William T.L. Armstrong (the architect of the first addition to the Nutley Public Library), who taught design.

At age 80, Mrs. Armstrong was honored with a special citation from NYU.

The Montclair Art Museum became her professional home after she left NYU in 1943. Her "Oriental Poppies" is in the museum's permanent collection. A bust of Abraham Lincoln that her third cousin began and was finished by her, stands in the Capitol Rotunda in Washington, D.C.

Armstrong studied art in California, Chicago and New York at the Art Student League. She spent several years as a pupil of William Merritt Chase, who was considered one of America's greatest artists.

Sources: The Nutley Women's History Month Committee, March 2002; Notable Nutley Women, Women's History Panel, March 2014.

Elise H. Yorton

Elise H. Yorton (Feb. 22, 1907 to July 2, 2001) spent the greater part of 45 years as a volunteer who hoped to strengthen Nutley's community character, a town she called "a friendly and delightful place, a town where you could cultivate yourself, help others and enjoy life."

Originally from Tennessee, she moved to Nutley and became affiliated with numerous organizations including the NJ State Board of Education. Her volunteer efforts have been especially noticed in work with the Nutley

Public Library and the League of Women Voters where she served as president before moving on to serve on the state board.

Yorton served as a trustee of the Family Service Bureau, president of the American Association of University Women, a worker in the town's recycling program, chairman of the Red Cross Chapter's 100th anniversary fund drive and centennial celebration, and a member and past chairman of the Essex County Review Board for Children in Placement.

For nearly 20 years, she served as chairman of the mayor's committee for United Nations Day and organized several bus trips for large delegations from Nutley to special U.N. sessions. She also organized UNICEF programs and fund drives in town.

In 1990, she was the recipient of the Mattia Award for Distinguished Community Service. Yorton said the award held special meaning to her because she knew Dr. Virginius Mattia in the 1960s through his various volunteer projects in town.

Sources: The Nutley Women's History Month Committee, March 2002; Notable Nutley Women, Women's History Panel, March 2014; Mattia Awards; Ancestry.com. U.S., Social Security Death Index, 1935-2014 [database on-line]. Provo, UT, USA: Ancestry.com Operations Inc., 2014.

Alice Lester

Alice B. Lester summed up her more than 40 years of dedicated community volunteer work: "Growing up in New England implants a conscience which directs one to become involved with volunteer work. Nutley provided the opportunities for service."

Lester began her career as a volunteer in a traditional manner – as the leader of her daughter's Brownie Girl Scout troop. Her older daughter, Dorice, was knitting afghan squares in a troop project to make robes for the veterans' hospital. The mothers were asked to help and Dorice volunteered her mother. As a child, Alice had been involved in a similar project for World War I veterans and she remembered the positive feelings she had at that time of being able to give something to the soldiers who gave so much.

This was the beginning of her years of service with the Girl Scouts. The list of offices she held and awards received are too numerous to list except one: she is the recipient of the THANKS Badge, the highest award given to an adult who has performed outstanding service to the Girl Scouts.

For most, intensive activity in one organization such as GSA would be enough. But in 1962, Lester became active in the Nutley Red Cross Blood Service and served as its chairperson. In that position she recruited, trained and directed the Blood Service volunteers and organized and ran the blood drives.

Following graduation from Simmons College in Boston in 1929, Lester came alone to the New York metropolitan area to interview for jobs. The offer she chose was secretary to the president of Fidelity Union Tittle and Mortgage Company. There she met her husband Theodore who later became assistant general counsel of Mutual Benefit Life Insurance. The Lesters have three children, Dorice, David, and Susan.

Lester received the Dr. Virginius Mattia Distinguished Community Service Award in 1986.

Source: Mattia Awards.

Joyce R. Donadio

Joyce Donadio's first visit to St. Joseph's Children's Center was simply to lend a hand to her husband and a small group from the Elks Lodge in Nutley who had organized a small picnic to cheer up the abused children being cared for at the Totowa facility.

"I went along to help with the barbecue but what I found was a disaster. Beds were broken, screens were hanging off the windows. It was terrible. As I was looking around and watching the children, I was thinking all the while that these kids just needed a hug and someone to listen to their stories. So I started visiting the kids on their birthdays and would bring a birthday cake. And then, one day I said to myself, "You know, I'm going to start an organizations to help, not only help for the abused children, but for all children who have special needs of one form or another. That when I started the Nutley Friends of Abused and Special Children."

Seventeen years and one heart quadruple by-pass later, Joyce was still lending a smile and listening to children's stories. Her Nutley Friends of Abused and Special Children blossomed into an important part of the lives of hundreds of children. Financed to a large extent by an annual motorcycle run organized by the Nutley Patrolman's Benevolent Association and supported generously by the riding Blue Knights. All the riders return to Nutley to end the day at a children's benefit picnic in the park.

Donadio came to Nutley when her parents Mr. and Mrs. Daniel Bevere resettled from the family home in Newark. After her graduation from Nutley High School, Joyce worked as a secretary at Hoffman-LaRoche and was privileged to be among those who knew and worked with Dr. Virginius Mattia.

She retired after 18 years at Roche but soon found herself working for the Township of Nutley as an administrative assistant in the Dept. of Public Works. Donadio received the Dr. Virginius Mattia Distinguished Community Service Award in 2000. Donadio, 62, died Sept. 15, 2008.

Sources: Mattia Awards, Star-Ledger.

Josephine Baldino

Josephine S. Baldino was one of Nutley's hardest working volunteers and best known citizens. She was involved for many years with virtually every group and fund-raising effort in the community. Her list of civic activities included service on Nutley's Visiting Nurses Advisory Board and the township's Local Assistance Board.

She was active in fund drives for the American Red Cross, the Heart Fund, United Way and the American Cancer Society. In 1986, she received the Jaycees Award for Distinguished Service in Public Health and Safety, and in1993, she was honored by the Nutley Branch of the American Association of University Women as part of its Women in History Program.

She was named Women Auxiliary's Volunteer of the Year in 1977 and in 1983 received the award for "service above self." The Bureau again honored Josephine in 1991with the Honor Award for Service and a life membership in recognition of her vital contributions to the Bureau.

Baldino was a member and past president of the Friends of the Nutley Public Library, member of the Nutley High School Football Booster Club, Nutley Family Service Bureau's Board of Trustees, former co-chair of the Nutley Family Service Bureau's September Social, member of the Nutley Family Service Bureau Women's Auxiliary, having served as president, clerical secretary and chairman of the Bureau's fashion show, a volunteer at the Family Service Bureau's Thrift Shop and a member of the Steering Committee, member and former treasurer of the Nutley Republican Club.

Sources: The Nutley Women's History Month Committee, March 2002; Notable Nutley Women, Women's History Panel, March 2014.

Margaret Mountsier

Community activist Margaret Stevenson Mountsier (Jan. 20, 1902 to Aug. 10, 1998), a graduate of Westminster College, served as vice president of the Nutley Board of Education from 1946 until 1952. She was the founder of the township Special Education Program. The spouse of Silas Rush Mountsier, Jr., was a founding member of the Nutley Chapter of The American Red Cross and the Nutley Chapter of Planned Parenthood. She was a member of numerous local civic and charitable organizations.

In 1953, Mrs. Mountsier was recognized and named "New Jersey Mother of the Year" by a jury of the American Mothers Committee of the Golden Rule Foundation. She received the award at a luncheon in her honor. Beloved wife of the late S. Rush Mountsier, Jr.; she was the mother of Mrs. Sally Dietrick, Mrs. Elizabeth Diachun, Robert W., John S., Silas R. III, Stevenson, and William W. Mountsier.; also survived by 18 grandchildren and 39 great-grandchildren.

Sources: The Nutley Women's History Month Committee, March 2002; Notable Nutley Women, Women's History Panel, March 2014.

Catherine Danchak

Catherine C. Danchak was installed as the 92nd Exalted Ruler of Nutley Elks #1290 in April 2003. Danchak had been employed as a teacher in the Nutley school system for 32 years, the last nine as a science coordinator.

Both Catherine and her husband, Jerry, who also served as Exalted Ruler, were an active, integral part of the Nutley Elks since the 1970s.

She coordinated the community image brochure and the all-American lodge contest form. Nutley has won these contests many times, demonstrating to its fellow Elks the work Nutley Elks accomplishes for the community.

Danchak was been active in the ladies auxiliary for many years and served as its president from 1970 to 1980. She also served as the scholarship chairlady.

As a lodge member, she was active with youth activity committee, hoop shoot contest, student of the month, National Foundation Scholarship Program, chairperson of the Handicapped Children's Committee and secretary to the District Handicapped Children's Committee.

Prior to being installed as first woman Exalted Ruler in Nutley, she served as a lodge officer for two years. In 2001-2003, she was named "Officer of the Year" for her work as a Loyal Knight. In 2002-2003, she received an "Outstanding Member" Grand Exalted Ruler certificate for all the past work she had done for the lodge.

Sources: Nutley Elks; Nutley Sun.

Nancy Greulich

Nancy Greulich was best known lately for her alter ego as Annie Oakley expert where, dressed as Nutley's famous sharp-shooter, she would delight young and old with the truth about Oakley legends, Oakley's guns in the Nutley Museum collection, and Oakley's adventures here in Nutley.

Greulich served for many years as a board member of the Nutley Historical Society. During the 50 years she lived in Nutley she touched many lives and left her indelible mark.

She belonged to several dining groups, dog enthusiast groups and was very proud of her work with her therapy dog Casey who for 12 years visited hospitals, Kessler Rehabilitation facilities, handicapped classrooms and people's homes.

Greulich was always seen and heard in and around Nutley. She was a founding member of the Nutley Thriving Survivors, a member of the Women's Initiative of Nutley, past-president of the Nutley and Essex Republican Clubs, an elected Republican official, a member of the John H. Walker Memorial Fund, the John V. Kelly Foundation, and friends of the Nutley Library. Nancy received 2009 Jaycee's award for Civic Affairs.

Nancy served the Nutley Board of Education for 29 years as a teacher's aide and purchasing agent.

Source: Nutley Historical Society; Photo by Michael Gabriele

Lt. Alice M. Lynch

World War II Navy veteran Alice M. Lynch was the first woman grand marshal of the Nutley Memorial Day Parade and was named Nutley Veteran of the Year in 2016.

Lynch was a Navy Flight Corps Nurse during WW II, serving, among other places, in Guam, where she treated the casualties from the fighting in the South Pacific and the Philippines. When the war ended, she had attained the rank of lieutenant.

Born in Newark, NJ, Alice was the daughter of the late John and Alice (Paige) Owens. Mrs. Lynch was a graduate of Good Counsel High School in Newark, and Jersey City Medical Center School of Nursing.

When Alice returned to New Jersey, she went back to work in the board of education eye clinic, giving eye exams for children from the third to fourth grade.

She met and married her Marine Corps vet William Lynch. "We decided to move to Nutley when we had our children, since our apartment wasn't too keen on children," she said in 2016. The price? "Oh, it was about $1,200 in those days." Here, they raised three sons — William, John and Robert.

She was a member of the St. Mary's Altar Rosary Society, the Catholic Daughters of the Americas Court Gratia, the Nocturnal Adoration Society and the Nutley Irish American Club. Mr. Lynch passed away at age 88 in 2007, Alice passed away at age 97 in 2017.

Source: 97th Annual Memorial Day Parade program.

Margaret Rummel

Born in England, Margaret Thomas Rummel (1925 to 2017) moved to Nutley in 1947. She worked as a lab assistant at Hoffman LaRoche. She was active in community organizations. She served on the Nutley Family Services Bureau and was a Nutley election poll worker. She was a member of the Nutley AMVETS Auxiliary, volunteered for the monthly SYA luncheons, and was a past grand secretary of the Royal Arcanum Auxiliary.

In 2015, at age 90, she accepted the Department of Public Affairs Women's Advocacy Award from Nutley Commissioner Steven Rogers.

"Peggy" Rummel was chosen for her positive work in numerous fields, and for the impact she has had throughout a colorful, active life helping others. As part of the criteria for the award, this humble woman also served as a mentor and role model for younger women, dedicating years of her life to community service.

"Rummel has a long and distinguished history of serving our community and nation," noted Commissioner Steve Rogers. Her accomplishments throughout her life as she wore many hats shared a common thread: helping others.

"She was a Girl Scout leader for 10 years; served on Nutley Family Service Bureau Board for seven years, and since 1947 she has been a member of the AMVETS Women's Auxiliary and was the National President of the AMVETS Ladies Axillary from 1981-1982," said Commissioner Rogers. "Mrs. Rummel has also been committed to Special Young Adults for the past 34 years."

The award, she said, "represents an incredible journey over the past 70 plus years. I have had opportunities to do things, go places, and meet and work with some very dedicated volunteers."

Her adventures in service included taking a trip to the Montreal World's Fair in 1969 with the Girl Scouts, and camping with the scouts on their way home through the White Mountains; serving on the Family Service board and most of all, becoming deeply involved with AMVETS and the Special Young Adults.

Rummel said she joined the AMVETS team "because I met a very special young man from Nutley, named Nelson, who was stationed in England prior to D-Day. "It was through the Auxiliary that I met volunteers who were dedicated to serving the veterans and our community."

Nelson, who landed on Normandy Beach on D-Day, it turns out, became her beloved husband.

Sources: Diane Lilli, The Jersey Tomato; Nutley Department of Public Affairs.

Maxine Hoffer

Maxine (Larson) Hoffer taught English for 41 years at Nutley High School before retiring in June 1975. She chaired the English Department for 13 years before retiring. Along with Guy Tiene and Raymond Kohere, she developed the NHS Humanities program.

In 1972, she was first recipient of the Nutley Jaycees Distinguished Service Citizen Award for her contributions in the field of education. A graduate of Nutley High School, she often told how she was inspired by Miss Marion Walker, a pioneer in Nutley's educational system.

Hoffer contributed to many aspects of NHS and shared with her students not only her knowledge of English but Nutley history and her love of animals. She was full of enthusiasm interacting with young people, charm and she had a magnificent sense of humor. She was a graduate of Barnard College.

After she retired, Hoffer was a once a week guide at The Bronx Zoo as part of "The Friends of the Zoo", a volunteer educational arm of the New York Zoological Society. In Nutley she was always helping others with lost cats or finding homes for kittens.

Sources: Jeff Grieco, Nutley Jaycees.

Michele Fleitell

Lifelong Nutley resident Michelle Fleitell is a founder of Nutley Thriving Survivors. She has served as president since its inception in 2003. The organization is a support program for women who live or work in Nutley and have battled breast cancer. Each year they organize a walk and a brunch, attended by nearly 300 survivors and supporters. They provide food for those undergoing treatment, companionship and support to these women in need. Their major fundraiser is a golf tournament, from which all the money raised goes directly to support the organization.

Elected to two terms on the Nutley Board of Education, Fleitell is active in numerous community organizations. She is past president and chair of several committees for the Radcliffe PTA. She was active for years with the Nutley Family Service Bureau, she serves as a trustee on the board of directors. She is a past president, vice president, secretary and treasurer of the Nutley Family Service Women's Auxiliary. She also chaired the charity ball.

Fleitell earned her undergraduate and graduate degrees at Montclair State University. She served as a guidance director and supervisor with the Nutley Public Schools until her retirement in 2008. She and her husband Sam are owners of Trio Jewelers. They have two children, Rachel and Michael.

Source: The Jaycees Civic Affairs Award.

Sr. Romilda Chiga

In 1983, Sister Romilda Chiga received the Dr. Virginius Mattia Award for distinguished community service in Nutley only a few years after joining Holy Family Church and setting her goal as caring for as many children as possible so that sense of well-being can envelop their families. Sister Romilda and her fellow nuns cared for hundreds of youngsters through the years at Holy Family Nursery School.

She was born in Zollino, province of Lecce, Italy and baptized Maria Teresa Chiga, daughter of Giuseppe Chiga and Abbondanza Ferente. Upon entering the novitiate for her religious formation on November 19, 1956, she was given the religious name Sister Romilda of St. Joseph.

Arriving in the United States in 1958, she began six decades of religious service, professing her perpetual vows on December 10, 1962. She was assigned to various convents and schools, where she could continue her education locally at Mercy College in New York and Seton Hall University in New Jersey.

Upon attaining her New York and New Jersey teaching credentials, Sister Romilda returned to the convent in Jersey City, where she began her formal teaching assignment at St. Elizabeth Child Care Center. In the early 1980s Sister Romilda was transferred to Holy Family School in Nutley.

Local protests were held when it was learned Sister Romilda would be sent away from Holy Family Nursery School on mission work in Indonesia, India and Panama. While she may have been on the other side of the world, Sister Romilda was always in the hearts of the people of Nutley.

In October 2000, Sr. Romilda left for the Philippines to oversee a newly founded convent and where she managed the construction of a chapel for the convent.

Sister Romilda was honored locally as a recipient of the distinguished Knights of Columbus Santa Maria award; and named Grand Marshall of the Nutley Belleville Columbus Day Parade. Sister Romilda Chiga passed away on August 18, 2018.

Sources: S.W. Brown & Son Funeral Home, Inc.; Mattia Awards.

Maureen Marion

Maureen Marion, who passed away from colon cancer at the age of 38 after her second term as president with the Nutley Junior Women's Club, was a great inspiration to the club, as well as to the town. In addition to serving as president, she served as second vice president for membership for two years, first vice president for one year and federation secretary for one year.

She was also chairman for music, drama, public relations and public affairs departments. Most of all, she was instrumental, along with all the Juniors, in raising money through the Nutley Junior Women's Club to build the Parks and Recreation building and the Senior Complex at 44 Park Ave. in Nutley.

Marion personified the meaning of service and truly embodied the club's motto "Joy in Service, Pride in Achievement," according to members.

Sources: Nutley Junior Women's Club; Maureen Marion Memorial Scholarship Fund.

Anne Rotonda

Although best known for her work with Nutley's Special Young Adults organization, Anne E. Rotonda has been volunteering her time and energies since her freshman year at Nutley High School. Originally, she had hoped to go on and become a nurse and thus, quite appropriately, Annie served as president of Nutley's Youth for Age Club which in the 1970's met in the Elks Club. Appropriately, she also was president of Nutley High's Future Nurses Club at the same time.

But a change in her career goals came quite dramatically during Anne's sophomore year as a result of TV newsman Geraldo Rivera's graphic reports on the horrific conditions at the Willowbrook Institution for Children on Staten Island. Annie was so personally moved by Rivera's nightly news reports that she organized a clothing drive for the children.

Eventually, she persuaded someone with a U-Haul to carry the clothes to Staten Island. Annie went along for the ride – a ride that changed her life.

"I visited all the wards while I was there, and that's when I saw that little baby. She was blind and so dirty. And she smelled awful. When I tried to speak to her, the baby reached out to me with her deformed hand. I wanted to take her home then. I don't even remember her name today, but it was when I saw that little baby that I knew what I was going to do with my life."

Annie returned to Nutley and soon volunteered as much spare time as she had to helping out the teachers at the Special Education program which at that time was held at Lincoln School. She organized and then played in a series of benefit marathon softball games to help raise funds for the program. At the same time, she began volunteering weekends at Holy Family's Religious Educational Program for Handicapped Children. She eventually became the assistant director of the Holy Family program.

After her graduation from Nutley High, Anne earned degrees in special education and the teaching of handicapped children at Kean College

Annie continued to volunteer her time and special talents while an undergraduate at Kean College. For two years, she was the volunteer assistant recreation director at Cornell Hall, a nursing home in Roselle Park. She also was a volunteer teacher of trainable handicapped adolescents at Burnet Jr. High School in Union.

Following college graduation, Annie's volunteer activities centered around the then-fledgling Special Young Adults Organization in Nutley. Originally, the sessions were held at a variety of locations including the basement of the Public Safety Building and at the Parks and Recreation facility.

The Nutley SYA moved into its new home on Franklin Avenue in 1979. In 1980, Anne Rotonda was hired as director of the Special Young Adults. Annie has turned her work with the SYA into a 24-hour day commitment.

Sources: Mattia Awards; Anne Rotonda Interview.

Edith M. Hutchinson

Edith M. Hutchinson was a longtime resident of Nutley, living on the corner of Rutgers Place and North Road. Born in England, Miss Hutchinson came to the United States as a young girl. She graduated from Mt. Holyoke College. She was reporter with the old *Newark Evening News*, pioneering in coverage of women in politics. She was assigned to the New Jersey State Legislature for many years and won many awards for her fair and incisive reporting.

Sources: The Nutley Women's History Month Committee, March 2002; Notable Nutley Women, Women's History Panel, March 2014.

Rosalie Scheckel

Rosalie Scheckel moved to Nutley in 1965 and became active in numerous civic organizations. After serving on the Nutley Planning Board and Board of Adjustment she was elected to the board of education. She served as a BOE member for 12 years, two of which was served as president.

With a four year old son at home, and having endured the hardship of losing her husband, Scheckel, who had started her career in education, enrolled in Rutgers Law School. She graduated the same year her oldest son graduated from high school.

She is a practicing attorney and the head of the landlord tenant section of Feinstein, Raiss, Kelin & Booker, and serves on the Essex County bench-bar committee for the Special Civil Part and the Supreme Court Committee for practice in the Special Civil Part.

Sources: The Nutley Women's History Month Committee, March 2002; Notable Nutley Women, Women's History Panel, March 2014.

Florence E. Rutan

Florence Rutan, who was Nutley's township clerk for 22 years, started her 51 year tenure as municipal employee in 1916. She was hired as a clerk-stenographer and quickly moved from that position to assistant town clerk then to town clerk. In addition to being town clerk she also served as the town's tax collector for many years.

Rutan was a member of the Municipal Receivers, Tax Collectors and. Treasurers' Association of New Jersey as well as a member of the Municipal Finance Officers Association. Rutan was a charter member of the Tri-Town Business and Professional Women's Association, and the Nutley Historical Society.

She was one of the founders of the Rotary-Annes, the women's arm of the Rotary Club. When Rutan retired in 1967, township commissioners adopted a resolution commending Rutan as an "exemplary citizen of the town of Nutley".

These accolades were well-deserved as Rutan participated in many civic activities including the Nutley Chapter of the Red Cross and the Nutley Family Service Bureau.

Sources: Nutley Sun, Feb. 16, 1956; The Nutley Women's History Month Committee, March 2002; Notable Nutley Women, Women's History Panel, March 2014.

Elsie Ciccone

Little did Miss Elsie Ciccone realize in 1922 that more than 34 years after when her senior year typing teacher, the late Helen B. Hawkings, assigned her to help the new high school principal, George Mankey, during her free periods, that she would be embarking on a lifetime career as secretary to five high school principals.

In addition to Mankey, who was principal of the junior high school and the high school during his regime, she has served as secretary to Dr. Floyd E. Harshman, Dr. Howard G. Spalding, Dr. Ehud Priestly and principal, Edward F. Assmus.

In June (1956), Ciccone will have seen 6,650 Nutley High School graduates receive their diplomas, each one of which has passed through her hands. Prior to 1923, the total number of graduates of the high school was 393. Her first class, in 1923, numbered 45; this year's class will number a possible 276! These figures do not include those students who have left school sometime before graduation, with all of whom she has had some contact.

Before advent of the Guidance Department, Miss Ciccone, because of her association with the principal served as counselor to students seeking advice about college, nursing and business schools. She has been instrumental, in the past, in placing a great many students in business positions, and still does. As the years progressed, she has watched many of them advance to enviable positions.

Called the "house mother of the high school" because she has endeared herself to both the students and the faculty, Miss Ciccone is noticeably fond of young people and is interested in their problems and pleasures. Throughout the years, she has had students helping her in her the office, an experience which they have later found very helpful.

Among her outstanding student helpers were Helene Matt, later secretary to the president of George La Monte and Son, and Ruth Grey (Bedford), secretary to W. T. Grant, of New York, founder of the W. T. Grant stores.

In recent years the boys of the school have asked for the privilege of helping in the office, too, and Ciccone has allowed them to do certain jobs for her. At times the boys and girls debate on the merits of their performance in the office, but Ciccone is silent, for she feels that all the students do a good job.

Throughout the years Ciccone endeavored to treat each student fairly. She tried to emphasize that one cannot get something for nothing. "I wish I had a penny," she told *The Sun*, "for very student who has left school before graduation only to come back later and say, "I wish I had listened to you when I left school. If I had taken your advice I would never have left."

"Others have returned to tell me, 'I wish I had listened to you and worked harder when I was in school'" said Miss Ciccone. "My greatest satisfaction, though, has been in watching the accomplishments of all the graduates of Nutley High School, in college, life or the business world."

Source: Nancy White, Nutley Sun, March 22, 1956.

Bertha Clark

Bertha Clark imprinted Nutley with her years-long volunteerism. She served as president of the Nutley League of Women Voters, 1954-1956 and 1964-1966. She organized Nutley for Recycling in 1981.

Clark served on the board of trustees of William Paterson College, 1967-1975. She served as chair of the New Jersey Committee on Children and Youth for 1960 White House Conference.

In New Jersey, Clark was a member of Gov. Richard Hughes' Tax Advisory Committee, 1962-1963. And closer to home, Clark was president of Essex

County Unit of the New Jersey Association for Retarded Children, 1958-1960.

Sources: The Nutley Women's History Month Committee, March 2002; Notable Nutley Women, Women's History Panel, March 2014.

Mary Perrotta

Mary Perrotta was named 2012 Nutley Italian Woman of the Year. A life-long Nutley resident, she was a secondary teacher for 38 years before retiring from Nutley High School on July 1, 2012.

Perrotta is the daughter of Yolanda Liloia Perrotta, and the sister of Laura Perrotta Ross, also a retired educator, and the late Yolanda Perrotta Evans, Esq. She has many nieces, nephews and grandnieces, and is always at her happiest when they gather together in the tradition of her Italian heritage. As an Italian-American, she epitomizes the work ethic that Italians are known for as well as being interested in the arts that Italians have contributed to the world.

Perrotta has been presented with numerous honors and awards for her teaching. She was a recipient of the Nutley Jaycees Distinguished Education Award in 1992, the Star-Ledger Honored Teacher Award in 1998, the College of New Jersey Outstanding Educator in 2001, and the WKTU radio station Teacher That Makes the Grade Award in 2009.

She was an active member of her faculty, serving on many committees and in a variety of capacities. Among those activities were the Educators Round Table, the Faculty Senate, adviser to both the Latin and Spanish Honor Societies, and chaperone to the award-winning NHS Concert Choir .

She holds both a bachelor's degree in Spanish and French, and a master's degree in Spanish language and literature, both of which were awarded to her with honors. She has also studied at the University of Valencia in Spain.

Source: The Nutley-Belleville Columbus Day Parade Committee; The Observer.

Marilyn Craine

Marilyn Craine was the founder of FISH, a volunteer group organized to assist anyone in an emergency with emergency transportation, help in the home, child care, a meal, services for shut-ins, etc.

Sources: The Nutley Women's History Month Committee, March 2002; Notable Nutley Women, Women's History Panel, March 2014.

Bernadette A. Ferraro

Life-long Nutley resident Bernadette A. Ferraro is a courageous woman who overcame many obstacles to become a distinguished biomedical scientist. Dr. Ferraro holds several degrees including a Ph. D. and has authored or co-authored many valuable scientific papers. Dr. Ferraro was inducted into the Nutley Hall of Fame in 2015.

The daughter of the late Dominic and Josephine Ferraro, was graduated from The Lacordaire Academy in 1970. She attended Rutgers University majoring In Zoology with pre-medical requisites. At Rutgers, she was a Dean's List student, and member of the Rutgers Chapter of the Tri-Beta Biological Honor Society. After graduation, she was accepted into the University of Medicine and Dentistry of New Jersey, where her research interests included the pathologies of pulmonary carcinomas and brain tumors.

Post graduate, she was Education and Program Coordinator at UMDNJ Department of Pathology where she was a lecturer in Pathology and instructor in Pathology Laboratory Methods. As a result of her research interests and data collection, biomedical writing became an important part of her diverse professional repertoire.

Determined to help disabled physicians, scientists, medical, and graduate students achieve their professional goals, Dr. Ferraro established and founded The Ferraro Foundation for Science and The Disabled in 1997. Due to her extensive charitable activities, H.E. Lady (Dr.) Bernadette A. Ferraro, O.S.J., was elevated to full royal honors into the Hospitaller Order of St. John Knights of Malta in 1994.

After holding positions as Pathology Lecturer and Clinical Diagnostician at UMNDJ, and University Hospital, Lady Bernadette entered the joint Program at Old Dominion University and Eastern Virginia Medical School in Norfolk, Virginia. Here she received her M.S. in Medical Laboratory Sciences, and Ph.D. in Biomedical Sciences while simultaneously teaching as a professor. She also gained proficiency in the use of the Transmission Electron Microscope, and Scanning Electron Microscope thereby becoming an ultra-structuralist.

Lady Bernadette has an extensive history of charitable affiliations. At 15, she began as a volunteer at Clara Maass Memorial Hospital, working in both the Clinical Chemistry and Pathology Laboratories. Her humanitarian horizons expanded to include international charitable giving by volunteering for The Nargis Dutt Memorial Foundation, a charity dedicated to providing much needed medical equipment to fight cancer in the Indian subcontinent.

Her memberships in professional societies include: The N.Y. Academy of Sciences, The American Association for the Advancement of Science, American Society of Clinical Pathologists, American Society of Cytopathology, The Dana Alliance for Brain Initiatives, and the Wilson Center for Strategic and International Studies.

Sources: Nutley Hall of Fame; Nutley Sun, Nov. 30, 1995.

Reverend Jill C. Fenske

Reverend Jill C. Fenske was ordained by the Reformed Church in America in 1985. She was the first woman to be ordained by the Classis of Passaic Valley (a regional church body of the RCA). She has served as pastor of the Franklin Reformed Church in Nutley since 1991.

She received a BA in Sociology, minor in psychology from Hartwick College. She later earned a Master of Divinity and a Master of Theology in Pastoral Counseling from the Princeton Theological Seminary. She was pastor of the Old First Community Church in Passaic for four years.

Prior to her church call, Rev. Fenske was a social worker for six years, working with New Jersey state prison inmates, dependents and neglected adolescent girls and the chronic mental health population.

From 1992-1999, she served as a consultant to the Regional Synod of the Mid-Atlantics of the Reformed Church in America in the areas of Evangelism, Social Witness and Missional Church Development.

"I'm one of those people who loves what they do, and where they do it. Both the congregation and the community welcomed me with open arms when I arrived as the first woman clergy in town. I continue to be blessed by the work that I do, and the good folk that I do it with."

She is a member of doorjam, the house band at Franklin Reformed Church, and a volunteer at The Hillside Café. Reverend Fenske and her husband Martin Williams reside in Pompton Plains with their two children, Albert and Linnea.

Sources: Nutley Celebrates Women. The Nutley Women's History Month Committee, March 2002; Notable Nutley Women, Women's History Panel, March 2014.

Noel Phyllis Birkby

Noel Phyllis Birkby (Dec. 16, 1932 to April 13, 1994) was born in Nutley to Harold S. and Alice Green Birkby. As a child she began making drawings of cities and towns, proceeding to build miniature towns in her mother's garden.

With an early interest in architecture, she expressed interest in pursuing it by age 16. However, her career counselors told her that it was a study for men, and that women did not become architects.

In 1950 she entered the Women's College of the University of North Carolina to study fine art. In college she was described as a rabble rouser and it was during this time when she began to identify as bisexual.

Her senior year she was expelled for an incident stemming from beer drinking, however, Birkby believed she was expelled due to publicly expressing her love for a classmate: "I wasn't hiding my love for another woman, didn't think there was anything wrong with it." Struggles with her sexuality would cause her a "numbing misery" and she would return to New Jersey briefly before moving to New York City.

Birkby took night classes in architecture at Cooper Union and worked for architects Henry L. Horowitz and Seth Hiller. In 1963 she received her certificate in architecture. Working primarily as a secretary, she left New York to attend graduate school at Yale University.

At Yale, Birkby was one of six women in a student body of about 200. This gender gap forced Birkby to "rise above the female role" to prove her capability to succeed within her program and show herself as being as "good or better than the men." In 1966 she completed her Masters of Architecture.

After graduating, Birkby worked a designer for Davis Brody and Associates, from 1966 until 1972. She helped design and oversee construction of Waterside Houses, a residential neighborhood on the Hudson River, and the Long Island University Library Learning Center.

By 1972 she would have her own private practice, occasionally partnering with other firms. That year, Birkby was the founding member of the Alliance of Women in Architecture in New York and participated in the beginnings of the Archive of Women in Architecture.

In 1974 she co-founded, with Katrin Adam, Ellen Perry Berkeley, Bobbie Sue Hood, Marie I. Kennedy, Joan Forrester Sprague and Leslie Kanes Weisman, the Women's School of Planning and Architecture. The school was a summer school for women involved in environmental design.

Sources: Wikipedia contributors. "Phyllis Birkby." Wikipedia, The Free Encyclopedia. Wikipedia, The Free Encyclopedia, 8 May. 2018. Web. 15 May. 2018.

Franca Petracco

Franca Petracco was named 2013 Nutley Italian Woman of the Year. Born in Calabria, Italy, she was the youngest of six children of Rosina and Antonio Turano.

Her whole family came to live in Belleville in 1971. As the Turano family transitioned into their new way of life, the first thing their children had to do was learn English and prepare for school. It was difficult not knowing the language well, and the children endured some tough times, but all learned the language and embraced the American way, thanks to her parents doing whatever they could to support their family.

Franca participated in the Italian Heritage Club and took Italian classes throughout her education. Since her English greatly improved, she was able to help many relatives learn English which enabled them to qualify for U.S. citizenship. After high school, she worked many years in the restaurant business, managing her brother's restaurants.

Franca has played a major role in the community, volunteering with the Nutley Red Cross and multiple school functions and activities. She is fully committed to the students in the Nutley school district. She has been a quiet champion and was awarded "Volunteer of the Year" from the Nutley Board of Education for her participation in many booster clubs, sports teams and fundraisers. She is especially proud of her involvement of the annual "Adopt-A-Family" holiday program. It is her unspoken assistance that truly defines her true generosity.

Franca married Alphonse Petracco and together they worked long days and nights to grow their first deli into a successful business in Nutley. In 1991, they leased out the meat department at the Food-A-Rama on Washington Avenue. In 1995, they opened Al Petracco's Meats on Union Avenue, and in 1997, they opened Petracco & Sons on Bloomfield Avenue.

Her greatest joy is her family. She is very proud of her sons and her husband for all that they been able to accomplish. Franca has never forgotten her heritage and her family's humble beginnings when they came to this country. Her mindset is always on giving back to her community, her friends and anyone truly in need.

Sources: The Nutley-Belleville Columbus Day Parade Committee; Nutley Chamber of Commerce.

Sally Goodson

Sally Anne Goodson, was named as the recipient of the first Department of Public Affairs Women's Advocacy Award for her outstanding work in advocating for women's health, rights, empowerment and equality. Nutley Commissioner Steven Rogers presented the award to Goodson at a ceremony on International Women's Day, March 8, 2014.

Rogers cited Goodson's work through the AAUW and other local and state organizations has had profound positive impact on women in the township of Nutley, from high school students to elder Americans. He also added that her recent efforts in heightening human trafficking awareness locally was an educational experience for everyone who received the information she provided to township residents.

Goodson is member of a number of Nutley civic organizations and has received numerous awards including, Rotary Club of Nutley Member of the Year Award, June 2013; Giblin Association Public Service Award, NJ 2003; Essex County Board of Chosen Freeholders, NJ 1997; United Way of Essex and West Hudson, Newark, NJ 1987; Distinguished Service Jaycee Award, Nutley, NJ 1985; and Outstanding Young Women in America, New Jersey 1972.

Sources: Diane Lilli, The Jersey Tomato; Nutley Department of Public Affairs.

Frances L. Shannon

Frances L. Shannon was born in Brooklyn, NY, and was a otherwise a lifelong Nutley resident. She graduated from the New Jersey College for Women in 1934, receiving a Bachelor of Arts degree. She later obtained her teaching certification from the Newark Normal School. She was a school teacher in Singac for 38 years before retiring in 1974. She was featured in *Life Magazine* on Feb. 12, 1940, as one of the 25 prettiest teachers in America.

Sources: Nutley Celebrates Women. The Nutley Women's History Month Committee, March 2002; Notable Nutley Women, Women's History Panel, March 2014; Legacy.com

Mary Rubino Ryder

Mary Rubino Ryder was named 2014 Nutley Italian Woman of the Year. Ryder's parents, Helen Bergamo Rubino and Anthony Gaetan Rubino, were both first-generation Americans. She was one of nine children, with the Rubino family having eventually expanded to 22 grandchildren.

Ryder's grandparents were born in born in Naples, Calabria, and Sicily, and immigrated to the United States in the late 1800s. Her maternal grandfather, Alphonse Bergamo, married Graziella Sutera and owned and operated a homemade macaroni store in Newark's First Ward where they raised six children. Her paternal grandparents, Vincent Rubino and Annuziata Neri Rubino, raised seven children with six of the seven being boys who all served in World War II at the same time.

Ryder is actively involved in many community endeavors. She serves as an appointed member of the Nutley Zoning Board of Adjustment, the Nutley Family Service Bureau, and the Nutley Rotary. She is the co-chair of the Nutley High School Senior Fashion Show, and a member of the executive board of both the Nutley High School Baseball and Soccer Booster clubs. She served as president of Spring Garden PTO, chairperson of tricky trays, a Girl Scout leader, and a team mom for little league baseball and soccer. Additionally, she is an active member of commission and board of education elections, and has served on candidates committees and been a challenger for many elections.

Ryder is a licensed broker/sales associate. A graduate of Montclair State University who majored in business administration, she served as a financial analyst with Schering Plough for a decade until the birth of her first child. She is the proud mother of Marissa, Michael, and Lindsay. She was married to Michael Ryder for nearly 31 years until his passing.

Ryder also received many professional awards. She has garnered the Circle of Excellence Award annually since 1998, and most recently was qualified for Gold level for 2013. She also received the number one status for gross closed commission and units sold.

Source: The Nutley-Belleville Columbus Day Parade Committee.

Mel Priolo

Mel (Carmella) Priolo was named 2015 Nutley Italian Woman of the Year. She is actively involved in many community organizations, serving on the boards of directors, as treasurer for the Mike Geltrude Foundation, since its inception in 2006, and the John V. Kelly Memorial Foundation, since its inception in 2010.

Priolo was a member of Nutley Unico, where she served as treasurer. She has been a member of the Nutley High School Career Advisory Council since 2004 and is the coordinator for the student awards fundraiser.

She has assisted Nutley PBA Local No. 33 with its annual death and benefits donation drive for 20 plus years. In 2013, she was voted as an honorary member in the local and received a Silver State PBA Card.

Priolo began her banking career as a teller at Nutley Savings and works at the Bank of Nutley, a division of Pascack Community Bank, where she is the vice president and branch manager.

A Jersey City native, Priolo graduated from Bloomfield College with a Bachelor of Art in English and education. After graduating college, she moved to Nutley, where she raised her family. She has two sons, Phillip and Mark.

Source: The Nutley-Belleville Columbus Day Parade Committee.

Linda Buset

Linda Buset is a strong advocate for women's rights. A lifelong Nutley resident, she built a business out of her home and has kept up with the times through continuing education and as a volunteer with nearly every town group. In 2017, the Nutley Jaycees recognized this community activist with its Distinguished Service Award for Civic Affairs.

From her Nutley High school days to her mid-twenties, Buset worked for Frank Orechio at Nutley's Herald Publications. "Working for Orechio gave me the confidence to always reach for my dreams and never give up." She started her All Secretarial Services 30 years ago.

"When I left Herald Publications to start a family, I still wanted to work from home. That's when All Secretarial Services was formed."

Now known as Virtual Assist, her long-running start-up provides outsourcing for office tasks serving clients, primarily small and home businesses, in the New Jersey area.

"My true passion has always been marketing and public relations, so with Virtual Assist I can help my fellow community members and local entrepreneurs."

Buset has four generations living in Nutley, ranging in age from six years old to 97. "I love Nutley, I was raised here."

She volunteers her time and talents to many Nutley organizations. She is on the boards of the Nutley Chamber of Commerce, The Kingsland Manor Restoration Trust and Nutley Rotary.

Buset is more than an active member of the Chamber, she's on the board, in charge of publicity and social media, and on the social events committee.

She is a member of: Nutley Women's Networking Group, The Nutley League of Women Voters, The Nutley Historical Society, and the Nutley Municipal Alliance.

Buset is active with the VFW Auxiliary Post 493, Nutley Relay for Life committee member as co-chair of Survivor Tent; Scarpelli Civic Association – Walk for Autism.

There are few groups or causes Buset has not worked with. Here are a few that were forwarded anonymously: Spring Garden School – PTA president three years; communications chairperson four years; PTA secretary two years, Student Activities Committee, three years, class mother, six years; Vincent United Methodist Church – Sunday school teacher, 25 years; youth group advisor, 10 years; food pantry coordinator, 5 years; Habitat for Humanity, soup kitchen. Plus, Cub Scout den mother for both of her sons;

Clara Maass Hospital volunteer, HackensackUMC/Mountainside Hospital volunteer, and Fernwood Dog Rescue.

Buset and her husband of 45-plus years, Bruno "Butch" Buset, are the parents of three children and grandparents of four.

Sources: Nutley Jaycees; Joseph Vendetti; Nutley Auto KIA interview, Voices of Nutley!

Susan Furnari

Dr. Susan Furnari is a product of the Nutley school system, as are her husband, New Jersey Superior Court Judge Garry J. Furnari, and their four children.

She has worked for Nutley School System since 1986 and has maintained an active private practice of psychology as well. In the past, sharing a passion for cheerleading with her daughters, she coached the Nutley High School cheerleaders and introduced a winter competition squad whose championship banner, presented by The Third Half Club, continues to hang in the gymnasium.

Dr. Furnari serves as co-advisor for The National Honor Society, is a member of the Superintendent's Advisory Committee, and coordinates Home Instruction services for the district.

She earned her undergraduate degree in Psychology from Montclair State University, her Master's Degree in School and Community Psychology from Seton Hall University, and her Doctoral Degree in School Psychology with a specialization in Program Evaluation from The Pennsylvania State University. In addition, Dr. Furnari is a New Jersey State Licensed psychologist.

Dr. Furnari is the proud parent of four adult children, GraceAnn, Melody, Angela and Garry.

Sources: Nutley Schools Special Services; Nutley High School; National Association of School Psychologists; New Jersey Special Education.

Laurie Cooper

In 1992, Laurie Cooper was appointed the first female volunteer firefighter in Nutley. An environmental engineer from Tulsa, Okla., Cooper served the department for a little more than one year before a job transfer required her resignation.

Sources: The Nutley Women's History Month Committee, March 2002; Notable Nutley Women, Women's History Panel, March 2014

Gail Ferrara

Gail Ferrara was Nutley's first policewoman. After raising three children, the lifelong Nutley resident returned to the work force and joined the Nutley Police Department in 1987. She is married to Natty Ferrara, who is also a Nutley police officer, currently assigned to the DARE program. She was promoted to sergeant on Aug. 23, 1999, and is the first and only female to hold that position.

Source: The Nutley Women's History Month Committee, March 2002; Notable Nutley Women, Women's History Panel, March

Captain Wendy J. Galloway

After a 27-year career as a Commanding Officer in the New Jersey State Police, Wendy J. Galloway was appointed Director of Public Safety for the Township of Plumsted in September 2017. As a civilian liaison to the Mayor and Township Committee, she will assist the police department with administrative duties, community outreach and sharing her extensive experience in law enforcement and government.

Her career started as a teacher and, through a variety of twists and turns, brought her to work with New Jersey's first lieutenant governor, with much to share along the way. She has achieved many firsts for women in New Jersey, and has actively served on many community boards, giving tirelessly to many causes.

Galloway, a graduate of the 99th State Police Class, retired from state service after a 27 year career as a Commanding Officer in the New Jersey State Police. She held many different positions as an enlisted member that included recruiting supervisor, public information officer and troop commander.

Her last assignment was working directly with the Superintendent as the Community Affairs Officer. She was the first woman to hold the post of spokesperson for the New Jersey State Police and is the first African-American woman to hold the rank of captain.

She was also one of the first women to attain the rank of major and is the humble recipient of numerous commendations and service awards. After retirement from the State Police, she worked three additional years with Lieutenant Governor Kim Guadagno as the Director of Programs for the NJ Department of State.

Galloway served on various boards and commissions such as first vice president of the Girls Scouts of the Jersey Shore, trustee for the State Police Memorial Association and a member of the NJSP Former Troopers Association. She is also a member of the International Association of Women Police and the National Association of Women Law Enforcement Executives.

Sources: The Nutley Women's History Month Committee, March 2002; Notable Nutley Women, Women's History Panel, March 2014; Ocean County Prosecutor's Office.

ARTISTS, MUSCIANS, WRITERS

Arthur Elder

Artist Arthur J. Elder lived at 90 Vreeland Avenue, Nutley, from about 1912 to 1920, having moved East after the San Francisco earthquake in 1906. The artist, known for landscapes and graphics, rented the Vreeland Avenue house where he lived with wife Ethel and son David. Their friend William McFee, an English writer of sea stories, lived with them from about 1912 through the time of the 1920 Census. It was noted that McFee's stay in town was one of his longest interludes ashore.

Born in London, England, on March 28, 1874, Elder joined the Chelsea Art Club and studied under prominent artists such as Walter Sickert and James Whistler.

At the time Elder lived in Nutley, the nearby Enclosure Artists' Colony was in its heyday. Just a short walk along the river and through the woods – soon to be Memorial Park – would have brought him in contact with artists such as Frederick Dana Marsh, Guy Pène du Bois, Albert Sterner, Earl Stetson, and Arthur Hoeber who while primarily a landscapist, wrote several books on 19th Century painting and was a critic and/or editor for *The New York Times, Illustrated American, New York Journal* and others.

After a few years in Nutley, Elder settled in Westport, Conn., in 1925. He painted two murals and three easel works for the WPA Federal Arts Project. He served a director of the Westport Art School until his death on June 28, 1948.

Sources: New Jersey State Archive; Trenton, NJ, USA; State Census of New Jersey, 1915; Reference Number: L-10; Film Number: 24; Ancestry.com. 1920 United States Federal Census [database on-line]. Provo, UT, USA: Ancestry.com Operations, Inc., 2010. Images reproduced by FamilySearch; WPA Artist's Work Card; Obituary, Hartford Courant, June 29, 1948; Who Was Who in American Art (1985), p. 184; Fielding's Dictionary of American Painters (1986), p. 255; AskART; http://ctstatelibrary.org/elder-arthur/; The Enclosure Artists' Colony, Nutley, NJ; http://www.livingplaces.com/NJ/Essex_County/Nutley_Township/Enclosure_Histo ric_District.html; Men who make our novels, https://archive.org/stream/menwhomakeourno00bald/menwhomakeourno00bald_djvu .txt; Nutley Historical Society.

Thomas Lovell

Cowboy artist Thomas Lovell was valedictorian of his the Nutley High School class of 1927. Lovell was born in New York City on February 5, 1909. His father, Henry S. Lovell Jr., was a telephone engineer. His mother was Edith Scott (Russell) Lovell. Brother Robert was two years older and his sister Margaret was three years younger. They lived at 39 Alexander Avenue, between Kingsland and High streets, in Nutley, NJ. The homes were later renumbered when the street was continued south across High Street, and while they later lived at 183 Alexander Avenue, it was the same house as earlier records.

When visiting the New York Museum of Natural History, he sketched the Native American weapons, clothing and artifacts. As class valedictorian, Lovell spoke on the "Ill Treatment of the American Indian by the U.S. Government," a harbinger of his depictions of the West. He attended Syracuse University from 1927 to 1931, where he earned a Bachelor of Fine Arts degree.

"I consider myself a storyteller with a brush. I try to place myself back in imagined situations that would make interesting and appealing pictures. I am intent on producing paintings that relate to the human experience," Lovell wrote.

Lovell was a well-known as an illustrator in New York City and as a painter of Western subjects. He paid great attention to details and seldom completed more than a dozen major oil paintings a year.

In 1934, Lovell married Gloyd "Pink" Simmons and moved to Norwalk, Conn. They had two children, David and Deborah. In 1940, Lovell moved to an artists' colony at Westport, where he became close friends with Harold Von Schmidt, John Clymer and Robert Loughweed.

Lovell spent almost 40 years as an illustrator and his work appeared in early pulp and popular magazines. His illustrations also appeared in *The National Geographic Magazine*, along with a series on the Vikings.

He produced several illustrations for the Civil War centennial series in *Life*

Magazine. Lovell's work illustrated many products, including the Continental Soldier, 1781, for the Continental Life Insurance Company.

In 1969, he left the world of illustrators and turned his attention to western art when the Abell-Hanger Foundation commissioned him to do a series of paintings depicting the southwest and early oil industry in the Permian Basin of West Texas.

Lovell was a founding member of the National Academy of Western Art. He won the prestigious Prix de West award twice for his paintings. He was inducted into the Society of Illustrators in 1974. In 1992, Lovell received the Lifetime Achievement Award from the National Cowboy Hall of Fame and the Robert Lougheed Memorial Award for Traditional Painter of Western History.

In 1972, he moved to Santa Fe, New Mexico. In 1977 he moved to a seven-acre site in Santa Fe and built an adobe house and studio.

Lovell, 88, died in a car crash in New Mexico on June 29, 1997. His daughter Deborah, 48, was also killed in the accident.

Sources: Tom Lovell Papers, Dickinson Research Center, National Cowboy and Western Heritage Museum, Oklahoma City, Oklahoma; Nutley Historical Society; Wikipedia contributors. "Tom Lovell." Wikipedia, The Free Encyclopedia. Wikipedia, The Free Encyclopedia, 4 Jul. 2018. Web. 16 Jul. 2018; John Demmer; Barry Lenson; https://www.illustrationhistory.org/artists/tom-lovell; https://www.pulpartists.com/Lovell.html; http://www.askart.com/artist/Tom_Lovell/7757/Tom_Lovell.aspx; http://www.fineartandyou.com/2014/02/30-glamorous-oil-paintings-by-tom.html.

Charles Nunzio

World-famous accordionist, teacher, composer, and arranger Charles Nunzio had a music studio in Newark and later at Nunzio Music Center, 401 Franklin Avenue in Nutley where he trained many champion accordionists who became successful professional artists.

He made his debut in a recital at New York's Town Hall in 1933, and an appearance in Carnegie Hall the following year. In 1938 Charles Nunzio became a founding board member of the American Accordionists Association along with Pietro Frosini, Abe Goldman, Sydney Dawson, Anthony Galla-Rini, Charles Magnante, Pietro Deiro, Gene Von Hallberg, Joe Biviano, John Gart, Sam Roland, and Byron Streep.

In the late 1930s he performed on an average of 35 radio shows a week on WOR, NBC, CBS and making commercial recordings for Decca, Victor, and Columbia. His 40-piece accordion orchestra won first prize at the 1939 New York World's Fair. He also performed with Guy Lombardo, Rudy Vallee, Meyer Davis, and Lester Lanin. In 1941, he published *The Complete Hanon* for the Accordion paperback, the essential book of finger exercises for accordion players.

During WW II he enlisted in the US Navy, where he played on coast-to-coast programs with the "Blue Jackets." Later, stationed at Bunker Hill Naval Air Station, Peru, Indiana, he assembled a six-piece orchestra, the "Melody Mates." They played three radio broadcasts weekly and all the dances for the Navy personnel.

A consummate performer, he received many awards, one of which summarized his 70-year career: "Presented to The Legendary Charles Nunzio in recognition of your contributions in developing the accordion's American Evolution as artist, teacher, composer, and innovator and as an inspiring idol to so many accordionists. The impact of your contributions will forever be felt."

Born on Oct. 30, 1912, in Sicily, he came to the U.S. at the age of 8 where his parents settled in Newark. He lived at 65 Oakley Terrace, Nutley. At age 97, he passed away on Oct. 19, 2010 and is buried at Holy Cross Cemetery, North Arlington.

Sources: Ancestry.com. U.S., Find A Grave Index, 1600s-Current [database on-line]. Provo, UT, USA: Ancestry.com Operations, Inc., 2012; http://accordions.com/charlesnunzio/#charles; Amazon.com; Ancestry.com. U.S. City Directories, 1822-1995 [database on-line]. Provo, UT, USA: Ancestry.com Operations, Inc., 2011.

William Pène du Bois

William Pène du Bois was born on May 9, 1916, in Nutley, NJ. His father, Guy Pène du Bois, was a noted art critic and painter known for his landscapes and portraits. When William was eight the family moved to France where he was educated at the Lycée Hoche at Versailles and the Lycée de Nice. They returned to Nutley when he was 14. After high school he accepted a scholarship to the Carnegie Technical School of Architecture; but college plans dissolved when he sold a book he wrote to pass the time during a vacation. In 1935, when he was nineteen, Thomas Nelson & Sons accepted *Elizabeth the Cow Ghost* and published it in 1936.

By the time he entered the army in March 1941 at age 24, he had written and illustrated five more books. He spent his Army years (1941–1945) with an artillery unit stationed in Bermuda. He worked as a correspondent for *Yank, the Army Weekly* published by the United States military during World War II. He also edited the camp newspaper and illustrated strategic maps.

He is best known for *The Twenty-One Balloons*, published by The Viking Press in April 1947, which earned him the Newbery Medal in 1948. He twice was runner-up for the Caldecott Medal. From 1953 to 1960, he was art editor of *The Paris Review*, working alongside founder and editor George Plimpton.

Pène du Bois married Jane Bouche, daughter of artist Louis Bouche, in 1943; they later divorced, and in 1955 he married theatrical designer Willa Kim. He died on February 5, 1993, in Nice, France

Sources: Wikipedia contributors. "William Pène du Bois." Wikipedia, The Free Encyclopedia. Wikipedia, The Free Encyclopedia, 6 Feb. 2018. Web. 16 Jul. 2018; Ancestry.com. Biography & Genealogy Master Index (BGMI) [database on-line]. Provo, UT, USA: Ancestry.com Operations, Inc., 2009; Wikipedia contributors. "Yank, the Army Weekly." Wikipedia, The Free Encyclopedia. Wikipedia, The Free Encyclopedia, 6 Jan. 2018. Web. 23 Jul. 2018.

Roylance Hall Sharp

Television pioneer Roylance Hall Sharp was born on Feb. 4, 1917, lived at 27 Brookfield Avenue in Nutley, NJ, with his father, Archibald, his mother, Bessie, younger brother Richard, and older sister Janet.

Roy Sharp graduated Nutley High School Class of 1935. One of his early jobs was playing the organ for silent movies at the Franklin Theatre, 510 Franklin Avenue. In his lengthy career, he worked with both Howard Hughes and Jerry Lewis.

Sharp began his career as a page at NBC in New York City in 1944. He worked behind the scenes in network operations and eventually moved to Dumont Television Network where he honed his expertise in station relations and managing National networks.

He became executive vice president at a new network, Sports Network Incorporated. Their big break came in 1954, when ABC dropped Pebble Beach golf. Sports Network took over the broadcast rights and Sharp put together a national network for the tournament. The company grew and grew, adding a variety of sporting events to its portfolio including golf, basketball, baseball and other events like the LOVE network for the Jerry Lewis Muscular Dystrophy Fundraiser which evolved into the annual telethon in 1968.

After Howard Hughes bought Sports Network Incorporated, forming Hughes Sports Network, Sharp continued to use his management and programming skills directly for MDA. He managed the network and station relations for the LOVE network for 30 years until his retirement in 1999.

He never let technology slow him down or stop him. In his later years, he embraced it, notes Lois Brouillard Knaster, "he even had his own Facebook page. Not only was he talented, but he was a really great person, loved by everyone he encountered."

Sharp was an accomplished pianist and theatre organ enthusiast. In his final years he enjoyed playing informally for his fellow residents at Brookdale PGI Assisted Living. Roy died peacefully at age 98, on September 12, 2015, in Punta Gorda, Florida. He was buried at sea.

Sources: Lois Brouillard Knaster; Ancestry.com. 1930 and 1940 United States Federal Census [database on-line]. Provo, UT, USA: Ancestry.com Operations, Inc., 2012; icscremationandfunerals.org; http://www.forevermissed.com/roylance-hall-sharp/; https://www.ancestry.com/1940-census/usa/New-Jersey/Roylance-Sharp_4q13zx.

Salvatore A. Asaro Jr.

Professional artist and illustrator Salvatore A. Asaro Jr., was born in 1933, in Passaic, NJ, and raised at 470 Harrison Street, Nutley. He graduated Nutley High School in 1951, and earned his Bachelor of Arts degree in fine arts and illustration from Pratt Institute.

Asaro was employed as an illustrator with RCA and General Electric, and later as a courtroom artist with CBS News in Philadelphia. He produced publicity artwork for the 1987 Broadway musical *The Wiz*. Among his many works, his portrait of Winston Churchill is displayed at Blenheim Castle in Oxford, England, and a tribute piece entitled "Forty Years of the U.S. Air Force" is part of the permanent collection at the Pentagon.

His artwork was displayed at the Nutley Museum and also in arts-in-the-park events at Yanticaw Park.

Asaro was a U.S. Navy veteran, an active member of the Hopewell community, serving as a councilman, and a former EMT with the Hopewell Volunteer Emergency Medical Unit and the Hopewell Volunteer Fire Department. He died at age 73 on June 21, 2016.

Sources: Mary Ann Fitton; Year: 1940; Census Place: Nutley, Essex, New Jersey; Roll: m-t0627-02338; Page: 7B; Enumeration District: 7-282; http://obits.nj.com/obituaries/starledger/obituary.aspx?pid=180400318#sthash.ayX wDDGV.dpuf.

David DiFrancesco

David DiFrancesco, a 1967 graduate of Nutley High School, is a photo scientist, inventor, cinematographer, and photographer. His contributions to the technical aspects of film making are truly outstanding. Most notably was his position as director of the Pixar Photoscience Team at Pixar Animation Studios. He earned two Scientific and Engineering Technical Academy Awards and has 16 patents.

DiFrancesco's early career in motorsports included road rallies, ice racing and Gymkhana's driving Porsches during the 1960s. He is a collector and restorer of vintage race cars and motorcycles. He has contributed to the creation of the Pixar Motorama, in what started as an employee-owned event that eventually inspired the creation of the film "Cars" and grew to an internationally recognized private car show at the Pixar headquarters in Emeryville, California.

As a photographer, DiFrancesco's work has been displayed at the MoMa in New York City, the Yale University Library collection, V&A CG collection London, England, and in a number of private collections. He holds a BFA from the University of Wisconsin-Superior. In 2000, he was awarded an honorary PhD from the University of Wisconsin-Superior.

DiFrancesco was inducted into the Nutley Hall of Fame in 2017.

Sources: Nutley Hall of Fame; Wikipedia contributors. "David DiFrancesco." Wikipedia, The Free Encyclopedia. Wikipedia, The Free Encyclopedia, 10 Apr. 2018. Web. 16 Jul. 2018.

David Gilbert

A Nutley resident since 1986, David Gilbert has had a long and illustrious musical career. He holds a master's degree from the Eastman School of Music, he is a virtuoso flutist and served as the principal member of that instrument with the United States Marine Corp Band.

His fame in the musical world was garnered mainly as a conductor. While he conducted many ensembles, most notably he won the 1970 Dmitri Mitropoulos International Conducting Competition, was assistant conductor of the New York Philharmonic and was principal conductor of the American Ballet Theatre.

From 1980 to 1982 he served as principal guest conductor of the Beijing Central Philharmonic and was instrumental in its rebuilding as the first American musician to hold a position of prominence in China.

His compositions for chamber ensemble, orchestra, and opera include his

"Concerto for Trombone, Brass and Orchestra," "Ballade Concertante for Tuba and Orchestra," and "Phoenix Madrigal" for flute and strings.

Gilbert was named to the Nutley Hall of Fame in 2017.

Sources: Nutley Hall of Fame; https://www.greenwichtime.com/local/article/The-Music-Man-David-Gilbert-talks-about-4307098.php; https://bergenphilharmonic.org/musical-directors/.

Dick Kramer

In 1976, freelance illustrator Dick Kramer of 79 Mountainside Avenue, Nutley, NJ, garnered national attention when he received the heralded First Place Black and White Illustrator's Award for Excellence presented by the

International Association of Business.

The prize was given in recognition of a series of graphic representations sketched by the Nutley artist for the Bell Telephone System's house magazine. Kramer's award-winning series depicted thoughts expressed by youngsters concerning their impressions of what life was like for children during the American Revolution period.

"When the editors of the magazine put it all together," Kramer told the *Nutley Sun* at the time, "everyone associated with the publication knew it was a winner."

The art director of the Bell Periodical entered the drawings in an annual competition judged by a panel of experts in commercial agencies from Maine to Delaware.

"Everything just fell in place," Kramer said. "It's a particularly significant award since this is the most high-powered and competitive section of the art world in the United States."

"I wanted to be an artist since I was five years old," Kramer said. "It's a gift which can't be measured."

As of 1976, the artist lived in Nutley all of his life, and now with his wife, Jan, twin boys, Rich and Robby, and daughters Suzie and Katey.

"It's the perfect family for the unregimented type of profession I'm in," says Kramer. "When we have money, we all go out and spend it together. And when we're broke, we all sit home together."

Born in 1938 in Newark, Kramer grew up in Nutley. Here is his story, as he tells it in 2018:

"I was never a good student, I spent too much time drawing. It caused a lot of trouble for me and my family during my school years. I was constantly in trouble for not doing my work. I was too busy drawing.

"I left High School on my 17th birthday and joined the Navy. It was one of the best things that ever happened to me. I realized the terrible mistake I had made with my life and finished my education in the Navy. I also achieved the rank of Petty Officer 2nd class at the age of 19, the youngest in the Pacific Fleet at that time. I owe the Navy my life.

"After four years I was honorably discharged and returned to Nutley where I asked Ginny, the love of my life, to marry me. Thank God, she said yes. We have been married for 54 years and she is still my girlfriend. I am a blessed man.

"I began my art education the Newark School of Fine and Industrial Art in Newark, New Jersey. I transferred to The School of Visual Arts in New York City and finished my art education there. After working for a chain store doing pen and ink illustrations for their advertising publications, I decided to free-lance. We had $78.00 in the bank, four kids and I quit my full time job. Ginny always believed in me even though it was a terrible time as far as money was concerned. She never complained or told me to get a real job, my father in law told me that. Ginny has always been behind me, no matter what was happening.

"I then spent eight years as art director for ITT Avionics Division, a defense contractor. I found out that I wasn't meant to be in the corporate world and went back to free-lancing. We moved to Florida, spent eight years there and that's where my entire life changed.

"I met John Meyer. At that time he was the head of H&K Training Division. He approached me about doing a few drawings for a poster advertising their training facility in Sterling, Va.. I said yes and produced seven vignette drawings for the poster. It was a series of SWAT officers doing what they do so well. I didn't think much of it. The check cleared and I forgot about H&K.

"When the poster was distributed worldwide, the receptionist at H&K threatened to quit. The telephone lines lit up with SWAT officers from around the world wanting to know who was doing these drawings and how could they get copies. That was the beginning of our fabulous life.

"We literally started at our kitchen table. I produced four sketches, the first of hundreds and hundreds to come. The rest is history. Ginny and I have been all over the world, from England to Germany to Abudabi and Dubai and all over our wonderful United States. God has blessed us with a wonderful life filled with good friends in the SWAT community and corporate world. Half of our business is from our on-line sales of prints and half is from corporate commissions.

"I never tire of drawing, especially the SWAT/military world. Ginny and I admire and pray for all of the fabulous people we meet in our business. They are the brightest, bravest and best that our nation has to offer. Our hearts break when a police officer or young warrior dies in battle. We are all poorer for the loss of such wonderful young men and women. I feel honored to be so close to them and what they do. Every day they place their lives on the line so that we can enjoy the lives and freedoms we have. God bless each and every one of them and their families.

"People ask when I will retire or stop drawing. I reply that I want to die at the drawing board. I love what I do and can't imagine life without my art. I hope God will grant me many more years of drawing the people that Ginny and I love so much."

Dick Kramer Studios is located in Leesburg, Va. The studio specializes in military art prints for Army, Navy, Air Force and Marines. Kramer also creates art prints for police forces and firefighters.

Sources: Dick Kramer; Kramer Named Top International Illustrator, Nutley Sun Nov. 24, 1976; http://www.dickkramer.com/.

Barry Lenson

Author Barry Lenson grew up on The Enclosure, site of the Artists' Colony in Nutley, New Jersey, where the writing and music muses landed on his shoulder.

Lenson has co-authored and written more than a dozen books, including the Amazon.com Self-Help Bestseller *Good Stress, Bad Stress* and the novels *Saved* and *Distant Voices* (the first in a planned trilogy of operatic thrillers).

Lenson discovered classical music in a shoe repair shop in his home town of Nutley one Saturday afternoon in 1956. He was there with his dad to pick up a pair of shoes, the Texaco opera broadcast was on the radio and that sound got into his ears and started what has become – so far – a 60-year relationship with classical music.

An avid record collector at first, he started voice lessons at age 18 and then went to McGill University's Faculty of Music where he studied singing with Canadian baritone Jan Simons and opera with Luciano and Edith Della Pergola. He then went to the Yale School of Music, where he studied singing with Phyllis Curtin.

After Yale, Lenson headed to New York and managed the ensemble and chamber music program at the Manhattan School of Music. All the while, he was performing with small opera companies. One day a community newspaper hired him as music critic, and writing took over. In the years that followed, Lenson joined the editorial staffs of EIC Intelligence, Boardroom Reports, and the National Institute of Business Management, where he was senior editor for more than a decade. He also served as the editor in chief of the *The New York Opera Newsletter*, where he interviewed major singers, stage directors and conductors.

Barry and his wife have one daughter and live in New Jersey. They enjoy attending concerts and opera in New York. He serves as a Nutley Historical Society trustee and art director at The Nutley Museum. He also serves as a trustee at The Jewish Museum of New Jersey.

Barry curates exhibitions of works by his father Michael Lenson (1903-1971), a leading American realist painter who was the director of WPA mural installations for the state of New Jersey. He and his brother were often models in their dad's paintings.

Sources: Barry Lenson; WWW.specialtymetals.com; https://blog.classicalarchives.com/about-barry-lenson-blogger.

Larry Hunt

"Piano Man" Larry Hunt was born in in 1955 in Nutley and lived here until 1976. From the age of five, he became well known throughout Nutley for performing on the piano, tackling and mastering pieces of classical music that were technically extremely advanced for his young years.

At eight years old, he won a years' free piano lessons at the DeJon Academy for the Creative Arts in Nutley. Under Mrs. Lythe DeJon's tutelage, at 12 years old, he became the youngest American to complete all eight grades of London, England's Trinity College of Music's demanding piano and theory exams.

When Hunt was 13, besides constant physical and verbal abuse, his father took his piano lessons away, despite the fact that the boy was considered a prodigy on the instrument. He is working on an autobiography describing in part this conflicted time in his life. Hunt continued to practice, teaching himself how to play rock music as well as classical. He started composing songs and pieces at age 15. After four years of abuse, Larry ran away from home when he was 16.

Throughout high school, he was encouraged to pursue his music by Raymond Kohere, a beloved Nutley High School Music and Humanities teacher. When he was 17 Larry became good friends with another Nutley notable, Raphael Rudd. A year younger than Larry, Raphael told Larry shortly before his untimely death in 2002 that Larry was initially the leading influence, the first person in his life, who inspired him to want to become a musician.

Upon high school graduation, Larry received scholarships to attend the prestigious Manhattan School of Music. He attended the conservatory for two years, then dropped out for reasons including financial.

After working odd non-music jobs for three years, Hunt meanwhile taught himself jazz as well as other types of music and began working fulltime as a singing piano player. From 1977 to 1989, he gigged in NYC, Boston, Cape Cod, New Hampshire, Pennsylvania, Florida, and on cruise ships. From 1989 to 1993, he toured full-time in Norway, Ireland, Sweden, Finland, Scotland, Holland, and Spain.

In 2010, he decided that he'd had enough of living and working on the road, and returned to live in the Nutley area, after being away for nearly 30 years. He performs on weekends and was named Music Director at the Hope United Church of Christ in Allentown, Pa.

Hunt teaches piano and singing and enjoys sharing with his students his knowledge and experience traveling and working in the music and entertainment business.

Sources: Larry Hunt; PianoManLarryHunt.com.

Michael Volpe

Born on May 12, 1987, and raised in Nutley, NJ, Michael Volpe went through the Nutley school system. He is better known by his stage name Clams Casino, and as an American hip hop musician, record producer, and songwriter.

Volpe's official debut "EP Rainforest" was released through Tri Angle Records on June 27, 2011. His "Instrumentals" mixtape was released on March 7, 2011, followed by the release of "Instrumentals 2" on June 5, 2012, and "Instrumentals 3" on December 18, 2013. The mixtapes were distributed for free through his website.

Volpe contributed a score for *Locomotor*, a work choreographed by his cousin Stephen Petronio released on April 4, 2014. He released his debut studio album "32 Levels" through Columbia Records on July 15, 2016. He followed it up with his "Instrumentals 4" mixtape, released on June 26, 2017.

Volpe's music has been described as "[bringing] together conventional hip-hop drums, a sensitive ear for off-to-the-side melodies, and an overdose of oddly moving atmosphere." Associated genres include witch house and cloud rap.

Bobby Olivier, NJ Advance Media for NJ.com, wrote of Volpe, the "producer's dark, dreamy, and originally instrumental tracks have led him to collaborations with rap stars Vince Staples and ASAP Rocky, as well as millions of streams online, where his style – a bridge between hip-hop and house music sometimes labeled as "cloud rap" or "trillwave" – thrives on YouTube and Soundcloud."

Sources: https://en.wikipedia.org/wiki/Clams_Casino_(musician); How this Nutley artist became New Jersey's latest music pioneer, https://www.nj.com/entertainment/music/index.ssf/2016/12/how_a_nj_beat_master_is_serving_underground_cloud.html.

PUBLIC SERVICE

Hermanus Brown

Private Hermanus Brown was the first known soldier of Nutley to give his life in service to this new country. He is buried at the Dutch Reformed Church Cemetery alongside more than five dozen local American Revolution veterans. Nutley, at that time was part of Second River, which included Belleville.

The Second River (Belleville) Dutch Reformed Church served as the local military headquarters. The mostly Dutch village of Second River was a patriot stronghold. A guard was kept in the church steeple along with an old mortar (left over from the French and Indian War) to be fired if needed to alert the militia.

The local militia unit was commanded by Captain Abraham Speer whose farm was located along present day Chestnut Street in Nutley. Henry Brown lived in the Spring Garden section of town and served as a lieutenant in the 1st Regiment of the Essex County Militia.

The blast of the mortar in the middle of the night sent the men scurrying out of their beds and reaching for their muskets and powder horns. Under the cover of darkness, shortly after midnight on June 7, 1780, the colony of New Jersey was invaded by a massive army from New York. Commanded by German General Wilhelm von Knyphausen, the force of 3,000 German and 3,000 British soldiers landed in Elizabeth.

The church bells began to ring and the hundred men of the militia formed ranks quickly. Among them was Lt. Henry Brown, his 18 year old son Hermanus "Manus" who had just joined the militia, and Henry's cousins Isaac and John Brown. The company marched off under orders of Brigadier General Philip van Cortlandt, commanding officer of the Essex County Militia, to take up positions at Connecticut Farms (present day Union, NJ).

In the Battle of Connecticut Farms, General Washington issued an order that three regiments were to pursue the enemy from three different positions. General van Cortlandt was to take the Essex County militia and attack from the left flank, with the Continental Army and the Morris militia taking the center and right flanks.

The Americans pursued the retreating enemy across a sweeping meadow. Unknown to the Americans, hidden in the woods at the end of the meadow the enemy had set up a line of artillery to cover their retreat. As the militiamen and Continentals charged across the fields, a barrage of cannon fire rained down on them from the woods.

Private Hermanus Brown, only 18, musket in hand, bravely charged across the open field towards and against the world's most powerful army. The youthful Brown must have felt like fellow militiaman Ashbed Green, who described the fiery charge across the meadow, writing in his diary, "No thunderstorm I have ever witnessed, either in loudness of sound or the shaking of the earth, equaled what I saw and felt in crossing that meadow."

As the pursuit continued, in the hail of cannonballs, tragically one found its mark and tore into the young patriot killing him instantly. Private Brown's brief military career ended just twelve miles from his home.

Von Knyphausen and his men boarded their boats and returned to New York. The Americans gathered their wounded and dead. The dead were always buried on the battlefield. That is, unless they were close enough to home and there was someone to return the body. As fate would have it, Hermanus' father and cousins were there in the heat of the battle providing them with the sad opportunity of returning his body home for a proper burial.

Private Brown was buried in the cemetery of the Dutch church where he had been baptized eighteen years earlier on a cold December morning. His tombstone read, "Hermanus, son of Henry and Rachel Brown, died, 8 June, 1780, in the 18th year of his age."

The stone bore an epitaph that read "Behold me here, as you pass by, Who died for Liberty, From British tyrants now I'm free, My friends prepare to follow me". The war continued for three more years after his death.

He rests with more than sixty-six other Revolutionary War soldiers at the old Dutch Churchyard where their honored remains are remembered.

Sources: Michael Perrone, president of the Belleville Historical Society; Nutley Sons Honor Roll, Remembering the Men Who Paid for Our Freedom.

Ellery W. Stone

Nutley resident retired Rear Admiral Ellery Wheeler Stone, chief commissioner of the Allied military government in Italy during and after World War II and former vice president and director of International Telephone and Telegraphy Corp., lived at separate times in the Van Riper House and Kingsland Manor.

Born in Oakland, Calif., on. Jan. 14, 1894, Stone attended the University of California, majoring in electrical and radio engineering.

Stone's Navy career began in 1914, and he advanced through grades in the Naval Reserve to rear admiral in 1944. As a captain in 1943, he served as chief of staff to Vice Admiral William Glassford. He was appointed by the Combined Chiefs of Staff as chief commissioner of the Allied Control Commission and chief civil affairs officer of the Allied military government in Italy, serving from 1944 to 1947.

After concluding his military service in 1947, he headed the Commercial Cable Company, a subsidiary ITT, and later oversaw its American Cable and Radio Corporation division until 1958.

Stone was an internationally renowned authority on communications engineering. At the time of his retirement in June 1969, after completing 45 years of service in the ITT system, Stone was a vice president of ITT, chairman of the board of American Cable & Radio, vice chairman of the board of ITT Europe (Brussels) and director of various American and European ITT subsidiaries. He was a director of ITT from 1948 to 1968.

According to the 1948 Nutley Directory, Stone lived at 491 River Road, also known as the Van Riper Homestead which was part of the ITT campus. According to the 1952 Nutley Directory, Stone lived at 3

Kingsland Road, also known as Kingsland Manor. Stone, 87, died at Mountainside Hospital, Glen Ridge, on September 18, 1981.

Sources: 1948 Nutley Directory; 1952 Nutley Directory; Rear Admiral Stone Dead at 87; ITT Director, Military Governor, Nutley Sun, Sept. 18, 1981; Wikipedia contributors. "Ellery W. Stone." Wikipedia, The Free Encyclopedia. Wikipedia, The Free Encyclopedia, 5 Mar. 2017. Web. 23 Jul. 2018; Dorothy Greengrove; https://www.findagrave.com/memorial/62089638/ellery-w-stone.

Gerald Ferraro

Nutley Police Sergeant Gerald Michael Ferraro was tasked with collecting all the names, addresses, and information on newly arrived Italian immigrants as they settled in our town during the 1930s due to the turmoil in Europe at the time.

Authorities considered information gathering on newly arrived immigrants important to prevent spying and espionage. Sgt. Walter Raft was charged with similar activities on newly arrived German immigrants.

Sgts. Ferraro and Raft cooperated with the Federal Bureau of Investigation and their joint efforts were attributed to the safety of Nutley, and the vital transportation artery of northern New Jersey and New York City.

After the war, there was much competition and controversy as Ferraro was nominated for promotion to and would be the first Italian-American police captain in the town of Nutley. It was a close vote among the board of commissioners, and Commissioner Theodore DeMuro cast the deciding vote. Ferraro became the first Italian-American police captain in town on November 6, 1953. He held this position until his death on December 21, 1959.

The Ferraro family was among the first Italian immigrant families to settle in Nutley in the 1880s. Their family history includes the naming of Nicola Place after Capt. Ferraro's aunt Nicole (Ferraro) Steffanelli.

Sources: Dr. Bernadette A. Ferraro; Ancestry.com. 1940 United States Federal Census [database on-line]. Provo, UT, USA: Ancestry.com Operations, Inc., 2012; U.S. City Directories, 1822-1995 for Gerald M Ferraro; 1910 United States Federal Census for Jerry Ferraro.

Theodore Berger

Dr. Theodore James Berger, an osteopath, volunteered his time as team physician to the Nutley High football team from 1931 until 1941 when he had his first heart attack.

He moved his general practice office to Nutley in 1931, after practicing almost seven years at 77 Park Avenue in New York City. Born in Kirksville, Missouri, he was graduated from the Philadelphia College of Osteopathy in 1925.

Dr. Berger married Ellen Lois Miller in 1929. Ellen Berger served as an Essex County assemblywoman. The couple raised two daughters and a son in Nutley.

His hobbies included ham radio. He operated his first transmitter in New York in 1916. During one of the early expeditions to Antarctica by Admiral Richard E. Byrd, Dr. Berger received many transmissions from Little America when the regular receiving station operator in this country was unable to get the dispatches.

Dr. Berger enjoyed oil painting of outdoor scenes. He was a member of Grace Episcopal Church, the Nutley Rotary Club, the Nutley Speakers' Club, and the New Jersey and American Osteopathic societies.

Dr. Berger underwent open-heart surgery in 1955, and returned to the practice after the surgery. He continued his general practice here until his death in May of 1956.

Sources: Newark Evening News; Ted Berger.

Frank V. Tangorra

A Nutley resident for more than forty years, Frank V. Tangorra (1909-1983) served as a member of the Nutley Board of Education for nearly thirty years. His concern for the quality of education and schools went beyond the immediate community because he realized that for the local schools to be effective it was necessary to have a strong support system on the county and state level.

Tangorra served here as board president only four months, he quite literally was the "dean of the board," one of its most influential members for 29 years. In 1983, he was elected as the first Italian-American president of the Nutley Board of Education.

The *Nutley Sun* noted, "without question, Tangorra was the best mediator the board ever had in bringing compromise among conflicting forces and personalities."

Tangorra is credited with reactivating the Essex County School Board Association, which he served as president for three years. Under his leadership, the association became a strong force in both the county and state levels. The association by-laws were amended in order to enable Tangorra to continue for a third year as president.

His efforts were acknowledged by NJ Commissioner of Education Dr. Fred H. Burke, and State Board of Education President Paul Ricci. Burke appointed Tangorra to the Educational Improvement Center, N.E.

Tangorra also served as chairman of Nutley's United Fund Drive; co-founder and treasurer of the Nutley Adult School and on its board of directors; director of the Family Service Bureau; and, was active in the Boy Scouts.

In awarding Tangorra the 1979 Dr. Virginius Mattia Public Service Award, the committee cited that he exemplifies a person whose community dedication and service eminently qualifies him for the award.

Prior to his retirement in 1970, he was comptroller for the American Express in New York. As a certified public accountant, he also held financial positions with Schenley Industries.

Born in Rockford, Illinois, he lived in New York before meeting his wife, Jean, and moving to Nutley in 1937. The couple was married in Nutley's St.

Mary's Church. They raised three children here, Rosanna, Carol, and William. The sports field at Nutley Park Oval is named in his honor.

Sources: Nutley Sun, Aug. 25, 1983; Mattia Awards; Essex County Board of Chosen Freeholders.

Julio S. Balde

Julio S. Balde was born in Ílhavo, Portugal, in 1913, but found his way to become a Nutley notable person by giving years and years of service to Nutley Volunteer Emergency & Rescue Squad, and the Boy Scouts of America.

He lived in Newark before coming to Nutley in 1950. Balde joined the NVERS in 1962, and was honored as a 15-year member and 38-year associate member.

In 2016, at age 95, the Nutley Board of Commissioners honored Balde, who served more than 74 years as a Boy Scout. He had joined the scouts at 15 in 1928.

In 1942, Balde was a proud founder and original charter member of BSA Troop 102 at the Immaculate Heart of Mary Church, Newark.

As a leader, Balde taught more than 1,000 scouts survival skills and the importance of civic engagement. About 43 have achieved Eagle Scout status. He attended five national scout jamborees. In recognition of his dedication to scouting, he received the Silver Beaver Award, the highest award bestowed on a scout leader, in 1962. The troop disbanded in 2016, shortly after Balde celebrated his 95th birthday.

He was a carpenter and cabinet maker by trade and worked at Artly Inc., in Newark for forty-six years before retiring in 2002. Balde, 96, died at his Nutley home on February 7, 2018.

Sources: Nutley Board of Commissioners; Nutley Sun, Hasime Kukaj; The Star-Ledger, Barry Carter; photo courtesy Lou Mascitello.

August E. Negra

Lifelong Nutleyite August E. Negra dedicated his life to keeping its citizens safe while devoting his free time to recreation for local children as well as assisting veterans.

Negra was born in Nutley in 1920 to parents who had settled here in 1903. He went to Lincoln School, Park School, and was the president of the Nutley High Class of 1938. Nearly three decades later, his son Ron was president of NHS Class of 1965.

Negra received sports letters in baseball and basketball and remained an avid Nutley sports fan his entire life holding NHS football reserved seats for more than thirty years.

While serving in the U.S. Army, Negra was wounded in combat in the Rhineland in March 1945, one month ahead the end of World War II. His brother John's airplane was shot down over Yugoslavia and notification came to the Negra family that August was wounded and in a hospital and John was missing in action.

Nutley Chief of Police Charles Rummel attended local pick-up baseball and football games where he encouraged the young men, mostly veterans, to consider a career in law enforcement. Negra and his friends took the civil service test for amusement, but after passing, Negra decided to join. He enrolled in the Newark School of Criminology to further his law enforcement education.

During his second year on the force, he was the president of the PBA. In 1953, he was promoted to sergeant, and in 1962, he was promoted captain. As Chief of Detectives, he was responsible for restructuring expanding, and modernizing the detective bureau.

Negra was a PBA member for 28 years and awarded a lifetime membership. He was department recruiting officer, founded the Society of Investigators of Essex County, served as a member of the NJ Narcotic Enforcement Officers Association, and as an officer in the National Police Officers of America.

In supporting returning veterans, Negra was a founding and charter member of Nutley AMVETS Post 30. He was also a member of American Legion Post 70. He sponsored a child at Father Flanagan's Boys Town in Nebraska, and after decades of support, in 1971, he was named an Honorary Citizen of Boys Town.

Negra was a founding member of the Nutley Midget (now junior) Football League for players and cheerleaders in 1958. He was the organization's first president. He also served as a trustee of the Rheinheimer Boys Club. In 1950, and was a member and officer of the Third Half Club and Nutley Unico.

Sources: Nutley Sun; Ron Negra.

Thomas H. Booth

Lifelong Nutley resident Thomas Hayes Booth, (October 9, 1929 to September 22, 1991) was the youngest of four sons of plumber Francis N. Booth and the grandson of Horace N. Booth, Nutley's first police chief. His middle name Hayes comes from one of Nutley's first plumbers, Tom Hayes, who taught Francis the trade.

Booth joined the U.S. Air Force in 1950 and was a Korean War veteran. He married Audrey VanDerWende in 1958, and they had one son, Thomas J.

The family tale is that Francis said that his youngest son, Thomas, had two left hands and would never make it in the plumbing business, so the plumber's good friend, a local judge, put in a word that helped Thomas join the Nutley police department.

He considered it his patrolman's duty to help people. When called to a family dispute, he often took a personal interest and offered his counsel. He also served as the department's chaplain for a time. After his retirement from in 1989, he became a school crossing guard.

Booth served as a member of the Nutley Memorial Parkway Commission. He was a member of the Stuart E. Edgar Post 493 of the Veterans of Foreign Wars, the Elks Lodge 1290, and the American Legion Post 70. He also belonged to the Nutley Historical Society, and the Policemen's Benevolent Association Local 33. He was an early supporter of the Special Young Adults in Nutley.

Sources: Nutley Sun; Tom Booth.

Dominick A. Rubino

Dr. Dominick Anthony Rubino, M.D., was born and raised in Newark, and is the son of the late Rose (Neri) and Frank Rubino. He graduated from West Side High School and earned a Bachelor of Science in pre-med chemistry from Seton Hall University. After college, he was drafted into the Army and was stationed for two years at a medical field laboratory in Germany.

Upon discharge, Rubino came home to New Jersey and worked as a chemist at Kentile in North Plainfield, so that he could save money to attend medical school. Rubino was selected from a pool of 1,000 applicants to be one of 80 students admitted to the first class of the first medical school to be founded in the state of New Jersey, Seton Hall College of Medicine and Dentistry. The school later became the University of Medicine and Dentistry of New Jersey and is now known as the New Jersey Medical School.

After interning at Martland Medical Center, Newark, Rubino opened a medical office in Nutley. While maintaining his private practice, he also worked for a time as a company physician at Hoffmann-La Roche and served as medical director at ITT.

During his decades of practice in Nutley, he has been known for his quiet philanthropy and true concern for his patients. Over the years, he delivered many babies, cared for entire families, made numerous house calls, and even shoveled a patient's sidewalk while making a house call during a snow storm. Some patients who moved out of the area were so reluctant to leave his care that they continued to travel from as far away as Virginia to remain patients. His unassuming nature and quiet charity are a testament to his profession and his heritage. Rubino received the 2015 Italian Heritage Award.

Rubino resides in Nutley with his wife, Joan. They have six children and 10 grandchildren. Rubino is a parishioner at Holy Family Church where he serves as an usher. In his spare time he enjoys working on home repair projects and vacationing in Vermont.

Sources: 33rd Annual Nutley-Belleville Columbus Day Parade, 2015 Italian Heritage Award; The Nutley-Belleville Columbus Day and Italian Heritage Committee.

David Wilson

In 1974, lifelong Nutley resident David Wilson began his public service career by joining the Nutley Volunteer Emergency & Rescue Squad wher he become an Emergency Medical Technician, treasurer, training officer, day captain, and served on many committees. The highlight of this service was having his future wife Dianne on his crew. They married in 1982.

In 1985, Wilson's mechanical background from Lincoln Tech, public speaking, financial training, love of people and the need to make the world a better and safer place, all came together when Commissioner Carmen A. Orechio appointed him as Nutley Fire Department Fire Inspector.

As a certified fire inspector and sub code official, he also served as the deputy coordinator with Office of Emergency Management. As the local Damage Assessment Coordinator, Wilson arranged for more than two million dollars in FEMA and insurance grants that reimbursed Nutley for storm losses.

In 2007 he was promoted to lieutenant, retiring in 2010. Wilson created programs for preschoolers burn avoidance education, dorm fire safety, juvenile fire setter intervention, and senior citizen fire safety. He served five more years in Nutley Code Enforcement reviewing building plans and ensuring fire code compliance.

Wilson found that he enjoys writing and wrote monthly safety and preparedness articles for local newspapers, radio, and OBC TV. He is frequently seen on Joey Bee TV as 'Organic Gardening with Inspector Dave' teaching healthy, cost, and time-friendly backyard gardening. He is a contributor to *Nutley Neighbors* magazine, writing about township history, organic gardening and other topics.

In 2009, *Fire Engineering* published his feature "So You Want to Be a Fire Inspector?" He also contributed to *Firehouse* magazine. In 2018, Wilson published *Fire in Our Lives*, a full-length book of his stories, experience and advice based on his four decades in fire safety.

A deacon at Franklin Reformed Church, Wilson also served on the board of directors and other offices of the Nutley chapter of The American Red Cross. In 1980, he began working at H&R Block as a tax preparer, instructor, public information coordinator, office supervisor and specialist in IRS audits. He served as Nutley Board of Education Treasurer of School Monies for 27 years.

Wilson's volunteer efforts and professional service have been recognized by the Nutley Jaycees, Nutley Rotary, Knights of Columbus, American Red Cross, and NJ Citizens Alliance for Fire Safety.

Sources: Nutley Neighbors; David Wilson; Page Publishing.

Daniel Dwyer

One of Nutley's most notable residents has four legs. On October 3, 2011, a lightweight beagle stray was placed into a gas chamber in Florence, Alabama, along with seventeen other strays. Carbon monoxide was pumped into the chamber. When the chamber reopened, only that little beagle walked out.

That's where the little stray earned his name, Daniel, like in the Bible when Daniel walks out of the lion's den unharmed. This little dog, Daniel, dubbed the "Miracle Dog" alone, stepped into a future that would have more impact on the canine world than anyone ever would have expected.

Eleventh Hour Rescue, a group dedicated to saving canines from death row in high-kill shelters, retrieved the twenty-pound part-beagle and sought a forever home for him. In the meantime, the Randolph, NJ, based group arranged a foster home and visits to forever home.

Daniel's first taste of Jersey was during 'snow-tober' when up to ten inches of wet snow fell on leaf-laden trees in the surprise October storm. In Nutley, Daniel met Spartacus, who was part beagle like him, and an alpha personality. Shelby, a pit bull joined the visitor for a walk. Once inside the Nutley home, Daniel then met Rommel and Greta, two dachshunds.

At a visit a week later all five dogs got along even better than the first visit. And, a few days later, on November 10, 2011, Daniel arrived at his forever home with Joe and Geralynn Dwyer, and his new human siblings Jenna and Joe, in Nutley.

Daniel's story of survival provided a great opportunity to spread positive messages in general and he has become an ambassador for anti-gassing legislation, also known as "Daniel's Law" nationwide.

The Miracle Beagle is dedicated to encouraging families to adopt! Just like the canine brothers and sisters that he lives with, he went from being an "unwanted" dog to making his human and canine families very happy. Shelter dogs are good dogs and deserve a chance to spend their lives with a family in a mutually happy situation.

In the intervening years Daniel has spread the word about foster and rescue. His pals Spartacus, Rommel and Greta have crossed the rainbow bridge. But all were lucky dogs to share a loving home.

Because of this sweet pooch and his amazing story, Daniel's Dream Dog Rescue was created. The foster based rescue group uses Daniel's story to speak in schools about being more kind and compassionate in life. Its mission is to save every loving canine and place them with a caring family. Its vision is to save dogs before they end up in shelters by educating students and the community on compassion and kindness for animals. Daniel the Miracle Beagle sure is leaving some incredibly big paw prints in Nutley and elsewhere.

Sources: Joe Dwyer; Daniel the Miracle Beagle, www.danielthebeagle.com; Eleventh Hour Rescue, https://www.ehrdogs.org/; https://www.facebook.com/danielsdreamrescue/; http://noblestrength.life/; http://joedwyerspeaking.com; NJ.com, October snowstorm in NJ brings snow, traffic snarls, downed trees and power outages.

BUSINESS LEADERS

George and Elma Drewes

George Drewes started working with boys in his basement for therapy in 1956, teaching model plane building, flying, having a club and running contests. With his wife Elma, the family opened Drewes Recreation Supply at 285 Franklin Avenue, Nutley, in 1961.

Called 'Drewes Hobby Store' and located across the street from Nutley High School, the store was a magnet for everyone with free time in an era of crafting, budding technology, and promise.

Their store outfitted things to do for the family from kindergarten to senior citizens, including hobby supplies, balsa wood, parts and accessories for chemistry, science, trains, planes, model motoring, school projects, arts, crafts, mosaic stone art, paint-by-number, sports, fishing, camping, archery, skating and more.

George organized model car contests and held competition road racing every Wednesday night for prizes, and quarterly contests for prizes. Their in-store race track for Aurora model cars is legendary among boys and girls of that era. He was instrumental in Nutley Flying Aces and u-control gas powered airplanes.

The success of their business was based on personal service, satisfaction, savings, customer recommendations and an 'at-home' atmosphere.

Elma Drewes was the recipient of the Jaycees award for outstanding service by the public in 1977 and was given the Youth Service Award by the Nutley Red Cross in 1989.

George Drewes died in June 1978. His wife and fellow shop-keeper Elma died in 1990.

Sources: Bob Drewes; Nutley Sun; Ancestry.com.

George La Monte

In 1871, George T. La Monte obtained a patent for the manufacture of safety paper, and a new company was born in Franklin. The company employed as many as 300 Nutley residents, and its officers and executives played an important role in the town's affairs.

The national banking system instituted in 1863 had brought uniformity and validity to the paper money of the United States, which previously had been plagued by counterfeiting and confusion in the currency issued by state banks. The industry needed a device which would make checks and drafts drawn by a good maker on a good bank equally worthy of confidence wherever presented.

La Monte, after much experimentation, patented a simple idea which quickly proved to be acceptable. The process gave scientific protection to negotiable instruments that safeguarded them from alteration. He called his invention "National Safety Paper."

The company erected its first mill on Kingsland Road on May 18, 1897. The building, along a railroad siding and a tributary of the Third River, was a one-story structure measuring 100 by 50 feet. Three years later its size was increased twenty more feet. The mill ultimately grew to 600 by 900 feet, and a new shipping building had been constructed.

The latter day La Monte company was the result of experiments in safety paper conducted by the original La Monte and a paper company operated by J. and R. Kingsland. Until 1893, J. and R. Kingsland manufactured paper for Mr. La Monte who perfected experiments in safety paper at the Kingsland factory. In 1905, La Monte and his son, George M. La Monte, merged with the Kingsland Paper Mills. In 1931, the company moved its principle offices from New York to the Nutley mill.

Georgia Pacific acquired La Monte and Roche purchased the property from the Georgia Pacific Co. in 1968. In 2011, when the pharmaceutical firm left Nutley, the building was razed with some artifacts donated, including the 1871 cornerstone, to the Nutley Historical Society.

Sources: Frank J. Church, Nutley Yesterday Today, Ann Troy; Meghan Grant, Nutley Sun; Wikipedia contributors. "George M. La Monte." Wikipedia, The Free Encyclopedia. Wikipedia, The Free Encyclopedia, 22 Jul. 2018. Web. 7 Aug. 2018; Federal Corporation Information, Federal Corporation Information - 049085-7.

Emmanuel Atzeri

Emmanuel "Manny" Atzeri and his wife Jeannine Atzeri sold their confectionary store in Newark and purchased Town and Country Deli at 96 Centre Street in 1967, and operated the deli for 30 years until 1997.

All the food was homemade and it was a lot of work and long hours. Fortunately Manny and Jeannine both loved to cook and it they picked the perfect business to marry. The couple managed to work and live together 24 hours a day under some stressful and hard times, but wouldn't have traded a moment of it.

They were recognized for their hard work and the business they put together. As the years passed, their customers dropped the formal store name saying, "Oh, we have to go to Manny or Jeannine's Deli for their best homemade (fill in the blank – roast beef, Virginia ham, salads, subs, and sandwiches)!"

All the customers were on a first-name basis.

Their deli was a mini supermarket. It carried everything from paper products, can goods, ice cream, milk, bread, cakes, cookies, crackers, candy, fresh fruit and veggies, local and famous Brookdale soda in all flavors, cigarettes, imported meats and cheeses. Regular customers arrived early each morning for their buttered Zinicola rolls, and sandwiches with fresh brewed coffee!

Manny's sister, Marie, married Anthony Amico, an American soldier and relocated to America. Manny and Jeannine followed, living in Newark where their daughter Natalie was born, before settling in Nutley.

Manny and Jeannine arrived in New York from France in the late 1950s following a 21-day trip across the ocean. Although they barely spoke English, their ability to speak five languages, French, Italian, German, Spanish, and Portuguese, helped them communicate with various nationalities here and in their little shop. They attributed their fluency to playing a big role in helping them reach the America Dream.

Source: Natalie Atzeri

Anthony Biondi

Family is the key at the Biondi Funeral Home. Anthony A. Biondi and his wife Michelina "Mickey", Anthony Jr. and his spouse Lisa, "are the cornerstone of our family business we work together sacrificing everything. We never leave a family to a stranger. It's all BIONDI all the time," says Anthony Jr.

T
he Biondi Funeral Home is a third generation family-owned funeral home and a Nutley landmark for more than fifty years.

Alfred A. Biondi and his wife Anna founded the Biondi Funeral Home in the Ironbound section of Newark, in 1941. Anna became ill and passed away in 1952, at the young age of 37. Alfred, together with his son, Anthony continued to operate the funeral home until Alfred's passing in 1963.

In 1968, Anthony and Mickey opened the Biondi Funeral Home on Franklin Avenue in Nutley. The Newark funeral home closed in 1974 when the businesses were consolidated. As the years passed, and the need for services in the community increased, the building was completely remodeled and redecorated. Additional parking was added, as well as parking attendants in order to continue giving the highest quality service.

Anthony has been active in the community for more than 50 years as a member and past president of the Nutley Chapter of UNICO National, past president of the Nutley Italian-American Civic Association, past president of the Optimist Club of Nutley, member of Nutley Elks Lodge

#1290, and was actively involved with the Parish Council of Holy Family Church, also a member of the Nutley Township Shade Tree Commission.

Nutley native Anthony Jr. manages the funeral home. He is a member of the National Funeral Directors Association and NJ State Funeral Directors Association. He serves on the Nutley Shade Tree Committee which was founded by his dad and Commissioner Frank Cocchiola.

Anthony Jr., is actively involved in St. Mary's Knights of Columbus Council #2346, a member of the Nutley Rotary, an officer and member-at-large of Nutley UNICO, as well as a past officer of the Nutley Elks Lodge #1290.

Michelina "Mickey" is a member of Tri-Town Business and Professional Women's Club of Nutley, Belleville and Bloomfield, member of the Ladies' Auxiliary of the Elks Lodge #1290, and a member of the Nutley Opti-Mrs. She served as president for the St. Lucy Filippini Sodality of Holy Family Church, is a past member of the Parish Council for Holy Family Church, and past president of the Italian-American Civic Association Ladies' Auxiliary.

Lisa joined the business seven years ago and is a professional funeral assistant. She is active in different community affairs and is a member and volunteers in the United States Coast Guard auxiliary.

Sources: Anthony Biondi, Jr., https://www.biondifuneralhome.com/

Nick Cullari

Master mason Nick Cullari practiced his trade throughout town for more than 40 years. Cullari changed the face and landscape of Nutley, and other towns, taking great pride in his work and his trade.

Throughout Nutley, you may notice numerous houses and commercial buildings adorned in what is commonly known as field stone on the outside. The particular homes and buildings he worked on are lost to time, but Cullari was an artist in placing the randomly colored and shaped stones are set in cement.

Each batch of cement was mixed by hand and each stone set one at a time. His dedication and craftsmanship have withstood the test of time throughout Nutley and many surrounding towns.

Following his service in World War II, Nick married his sweetheart Helen, and was the proud father of daughters Helen and Joanna. The family resided in Nutley for the next sixty years. As a hobby he enjoyed painting landscapes, but his biggest joy was spending time with his grandchildren Dennis and Jessica.

Cullari passed away in 1999, however his widow and daughter still reside in Nutley, and his entire family are still very proud to say "that was one of pop's jobs".

Source: Joanna Cullari

Ottavio 'Tony' Palladino

For decades, locals would have thought D'Allessio was the last name of the

master tailor on High Street. In the early decades they would have been correct. But in 1977 when Ottavio 'Tony' Palladino bought the shop he kept the name of his father-in-law, the original D'Allessio master tailor, out of respect.

Born in Buccino, Campano, Italy, Palladino began learning his craft at age 10. In 1969, at 24, he left home and tried living in Chicago, but found that much too cold. But providence was with him when he headed to Newark where he met his wife Nevicella, Nella to all her friends, who was graduated from Barringer High School in 1962.

A long-time member of Holy Family parish, he and Nella raised their son Vincenzo in their modest home on Brown Street in the shadow of Lincoln

School. The youngster was born at Clara Maass hospital and he attended Nutley schools.

Customers knew to get their tailoring done before school let out. That's when Palladino and family would take six weeks to visit his siblings living in Italy. And while he passed on the store in 2018, he may not be retiring to Florida all too soon, not with his four grandchildren so close to their Nutley roots. So, keep an eye out for Tony's friendly smile in your travels.

Source: Ottavio 'Tony' Palladino.

Allen Robert Taylor

Engineer Allen Robert Taylor (1920 - 1985) patented the first 50,000 watt TV transmitter, and created the guidance system for both Apollo and the Viking Lander.

Taylor and his wife Georgiana lived at 235 Nutley Avenue, with their four sons, David, Keith, Tyson and Allen.

He was chief engineer at REL/Standard Electronics when he developed the transmitter. At Singer/Kearfott, he was a staff engineer and developed the guidance system for the Exocet anti-ship missile which was first successfully used in the Falklands War.

Among his many other patents are: Inflatable portable antenna system; Negative ion generator using an ultraviolet source to irradiate electrically conductive material (ion air cleaner); Broad band tuned amplifier circuit (50,000 watt transmitter); Filament lead-in and impedance matching structure for a grounded grid amplifier; Gyro autophase system (guidance system).

Georgina owned and operated a bed and breakfast in Ocean Grove from 1967-1985. Upon the death of her husband, she relocated to Daytona Beach, Fla, where she was a director for the Halifax Historical Society. She was an active volunteer at the Veterans Hospital, and a past president of the Maverick Condominium Association.

Sources: Allen Taylor; patents.google.com; Wikipedia contributors. "Exocet." Wikipedia, The Free Encyclopedia. Wikipedia, The Free Encyclopedia, 26 Aug. 2018. Web. 4 Oct. 2018; www.findagrave.com/cgi-

Samuel W. Brown

In 1950, Samuel W. Brown and his wife Anne, opened Samuel W. Brown Funeral Home in a two-family brick structure at 267 Centre Street. The building was purchased in 1949 from Mrs. Brown's uncle and aunt, Ralph and Angelica Jannarone. The first floor apartment was renovated to accommodate the funeral home, while the Browns resided on the second floor. A new facade and office were added in 1954.

In 1961, John F. Brown, son of Samuel and Anne Brown, became licensed as a practitioner of mortuary science, thus the name of the funeral home was changed to S.W. Brown & Son Funeral Home. Upon graduation from Seton Hall University in 1964, John joined the family business full time. In 1974, John and his wife Jo-Ann, purchased the business from Samuel. To this day, the independent business is family-owned.

In 1986, John purchased the Johnesee Nutley Home for Funerals from Everett and Mary Jayne Johnesee. Peter Brown, son of John and Jo-Ann (Di Iorio) Brown, the third generation Brown, graduated from Xavier University in 1989. He completed Mortuary College and join the family business full time in 1992.

Nutley natives John and Jo-Ann were in the Nutley High School class of 1958 class. Their first date was the Senior Prom. Six years later they were married by Msgr. Anthony DeLuca at Holy Family Church.

Jo-Ann volunteered for a quarter century at the Nutley Family Service Bureau Thrift Shop. She also served on the board and as president of the women's auxiliary. She has been active in the St. Lucy Filippini Sodality and the Rosary Altar Society at Holy Family Church, and many other local groups.

John was a member and served as past president of the Nutley Kiwanis Club, Nutley Lions Club, Nutley Elks Lodge 1290, Nutley UNICO. He received the Nutley Elks Citizen of the Year Award and the Nutley Police Benevolent Association's Citizen of the Year Award.

Jo-Ann and John also shared the Nutley Jaycees Distinguished Service Award in 1997. They received the Dr. Virginius Mattia Distinguished Community Service Award in 2004.

Samuel W. Brown passed away peacefully on July 27, 2008, in his apartment above the funeral home. Born in Newark, he lived in Belleville before moving to Nutley in 1938. A graduate of the New York School of Embalming and Restorative Art, Sam was the founder of the Samuel W. Brown Funeral Home in 1950.

In 1956, the one-family stucco residence, on the west side of the funeral home, was purchased and in 1959, the two buildings were joined together. Over the years there have been alterations creating the appearance that the funeral home is one building. The interior was made more functional and spacious with each improvement.

Sources: Mattia Awards; https://www.swbrownandson.com/

Giacomo Pontoriero

Giacomo Pontoriero was named 2013 Nutley Italian Man of the Year. He immigrated from Spilinga, Calabria, Italy, to the Ironbound section in Newark in 1966, and later settled in Nutley. His decades of construction and masonry work resulted in more than 200 custom-built homes in New Jersey.

With his partner Joe Fornarotto of Belleville, they were the driving force behind the creation and construction of the Belleville-Nutley Disabled American Veterans Chapter 22 memorial building on Mill Street in Belleville. The men donated endless hours and resources in getting this building completed. Veterans associations honored Pontoriero with multiple awards for his dedication and commitment to erecting a building honoring the disabled veterans.

The long-time Nutley resident uses his talents to help the Roman Catholic churches in New Jersey assisting with their construction needs. He was intricately involved in the fundraising and banquets with his close friend,

Bishop Di Marzio, for breast cancer research. They were successful in raising well over $100,000. The builder has been a champion providing much help and support to local churches, especially Holy Family Church.

He is actively involved with many groups and organizations volunteering both his time and money to assist the needy. He takes great pride in creating and designing shrines for his favorite saints within the church, especially his patron saint, Madonna Della Fontana displayed at Our Lady of Mount Carmel Church in Newark.

Sources: The Nutley-Belleville Columbus Day Parade Committee;
https://patch.com/new-jersey/belleville/dav-building-named-after-cdr-joe-fornarotto;
https://www.davnj.org/disabled-veterans.html;
http://bellevillesons.com/bel_dav_building.html.

Keith Jaret

Keith Jaret introduced Nutley to lingonberries at the innovative Petite Café

he and wife Maureen opened on Franklin Avenue. His creative palate led to new and strange-to-Nutley meals with unusual and favored new tastes.

The couple later switched from dinners to desserts when they opened Jaret's Stuffed Cupcakes. Keith, a 1980 graduate of the Culinary Institute of America, constantly devised, developed and created new and exciting hybrid stuffed cupcakes.

The New York media soon discovered their stuffed cupcakes and Oprah Winfrey touted their exciting concoctions. The business expanded to new stores in Hoboken and Endicott, N.Y., and the brand was distributed throughout the region.

"The cupcake fad may have quieted down a bit," he told *The Record* in a 2015 interview, "but it's still huge. People want them as favors for weddings. They want them for parties. They want them as a pick-me-up on their way home from work."

Former colleague Marc Mangano, an intern cupcake maker, described Jaret – a Grateful Dead-loving former "hippie" with tattoos on his arms – as the "rock and roll chef." He was also sometimes called the "Cupcake Dude."

In 1991, while awaiting a heart transplant, the Jarets' infant daughter Megan was named the NJ State PBA Poster Child. On Sept. 13, Megan received a heart transplant. Hers was the most successful pediatric heart transplant in Columbia Presbyterian history. It was the hospital's 20th transplant. While Megan's body did not reject the transplant heart, she developed a rare infection which took her life on Oct. 23.

The couple strongly supported organ donor programs. In 2011, Maureen donated a kidney that enabled a long-time customer, Dennis Paserchia, to receive a kidney transplant.

Keith passed away on February 8, 2018, while awaiting a liver transplant. He contracted Hepatitis C from a blood transfusion following a serious injury when he was a teenager. His treatments led to cirrhosis of the liver and cancer.

Sources: John Lee, TapIntoNutley; Eric Kiefer, Patch; Joshua Jongsma, NorthJersey Media; Anthony Biondi, Jr., https://www.biondifuneralhome.com/; Nutley Notables: The men and women who made a memorable impact on our home town, Nutley, New Jersey.

Keith Taylor

Executive Chef Keith Taylor says he's "just a lucky kid from Nutley, NJ"

Taylor founded Chefsoul Culinary Enterprises in 1991, after attending Cornell and The Culinary Arts Institute and successfully establishing himself in major restaurants in Manhattan. Classically trained and also known as a master of contemporary southern cuisine, classical and continental fusion, he is known as an expert in culinary operations and is highly sought after for his professional talents.

Ask him about growing up here, then simply sit back.

Taylor grew up in his grandmother's house on Kierstead Avenue. He attended Holy Family School and Lincoln School, and loved his neighborhood crew. He played baseball in the American Little League, and considered DeMuro his home park and enjoyed summer activities with Mike Geltrude.

The chef recalls the neighborhood families, friends, and local deli culture that influenced his desire to become a culinary professional. His first kitchen job was cooking as a teen at Yesterdays Bar and Grille, and The Sandalwood Restaurant at the Ramada Inn, both across the border in Clifton. He also enjoyed part-time work at Santini's in town.

Taylor says his favorite pizza will always be Ralph's followed closely by Ritacco's and the now closed Scotto's. He says, "Living in the center of the universe and the immigrant Italian culture played a huge role in my desire to learn more about food, second only to the influence and support of my family."

School days in town are fresh in Taylor's memory. "Nutley High School Class of 1982 was a big launching point with great memories and district teachers and administrators like Stephen Parigi, Frank Commune, Kathy Yates, Mr. John Walker, Mr. Suff (Jack Suffren), Jeri Cohn, Dianne DeRosa, and Phil Perello. They all have some responsibility for my love of education and Nutley schools."

It's no surprise that Taylor recognizes his early influences. "I must add that I always had a lot of love and respect for "lunch ladies" that I always thought did a great job, from Holy family School and Lincoln, to Franklin School and the Nutley High School cafeteria teams. They did it right for years providing nutrient dense meals that were made with love by local women who cared in ways that I do not see in school dining today."

Before attending college, Taylor served as an Army Ranger and a proud member of the 82nd Airborne Division in Ft Bragg, N.C. He didn't cook in the Army, he says, but he did jump out of perfectly good airplanes.

His experience is with restaurants, hotels, and organizations such as Walt Disney World's Restaurant and Resorts Division, Hilton Hotels, Restaurant Associates, ARAMARK Corporation/Sports and Entertainment Division, Bon Appétit, specialty resort engagements and as an executive chef of retail operations.

As a proven motivational leader, Taylor has re-tooled failing operations and successfully executed restaurant food and beverage openings in both private and corporate sectors. Aside from extensive management experience and proven operations systems, he has a strong supporting network of professional managers, chefs and industry professionals.

Taylor is planning to launch a national franchise based on Zachary's Soul food and critically acclaimed barbecue. He's also in post-production for a new television series about the franchise launch.

The short answer, "Chef life is good." He's a happy husband and father to four super kids. And, he is proud of his Nutley foundation.

Sources: Keith Taylor; http://chefsoulculinary.com/chefsoul/bio/.

SPORTS

Milton O'Connell

Professional football player Milton Timothy O'Connell was born on November 12, 1900, in Nutley, NJ. He lived with his father, Timothy, mother, Mary, brother John and sister Katherine at 357 Passaic Avenue. He attended high school in Easton, Pa. At six-foot, 175 pounds, O'Connell attended Lafayette University, a liberal arts college also in Easton.

O'Connell played in fifteen games in his National Football League career from 1924 to 1925 with the Frankford Yellow Jackets. He accounted for 6 points in his professional career.

O'Connell, 27, died on May 18, 1928 in Wilmington, Delaware. He is buried at Union Cemetery, Hackettstown, New Jersey.

Sources: Ancestry.com. 1910 United States Federal Census [database on-line]. Lehi, UT, USA: Ancestry.com Operations Inc., 2006; Wikipedia contributors. "Lafayette University." Wikipedia, The Free Encyclopedia. Wikipedia, The Free Encyclopedia, 6 Oct. 2015. Web. 24 Jul. 2018; http://www.pro-football-reference.com/players/O/OConMi20/touchdowns/; https://www.profootballarchives.com/playero/ocon00600.html; http://www.nfl.com/player/milto'connell/2522364/careerstats; https://www.statscrew.com/football/stats/p-oconnmil001; Ancestry.com. U.S., Find A Grave Index, 1600s-Current [database on-line]. Provo, UT, USA: Ancestry.com Operations, Inc., 2012.

Frank Kirkleski

Professional football player Frank William Kirkleski was born on May 19, 1904, in Nutley, NJ. The son of Charles and Josephine, Frank lived with step-brother Alfred Burmki, sisters Julia, Josephine and Helen, and aunts Annie and Blanche at 103 Harrison Street.

Kirkleski graduated Nutley High School class of 1923. He was inducted into the Third Half Club Nutley High School Hall of Fame in 1988.

A quick and powerful athlete, he distinguished himself as a member of the Nutley High School football team alongside Jack Speary, another local legend. He also played basketball and baseball. Frank was recruited by coach Jock Sutherland of Lafayette College, a disciple of Pop Warner. He loved the way "Kirk" plowed through his tackles.

Kirkleski was five-feet, ten inches and 179 pounds. He played college football for Lafayette College, Easton, Pa., where he earned a degree in 1927. While at Lafayette, Kirkleski was known as a hard-hitting back. He played all four of his college years as a varsity halfback. He received second and third team All American honors from the New York Telegraph and The New York World in 1926.

After college Kirkleski played for the Pottsville Maroons of the National Football League. In his professional debut, Kirkleski threw two touchdown passes to lead the Maroons over the Buffalo Bisons 22-0. Then on October 16, 1927, he led his team down the field on three passes, where he recovered a fumble, by teammate Tony Latone, in the end zone to give the Maroons a last minute win over the Providence Steam Roller. Kirkleski would haunt Providence again in a rematch on November 24. In that game, he threw a 21 yard pass to Gus Kenneally to give Pottsville a 6-0 victory.

In 1928, Kirkleski joined the independent Orange Athletic Club from New Jersey. In 1929, he joined the Orange Tornadoes. Kirkleski's final year in professional football, in 1931, was spent with the Brooklyn Dodgers.

In 2001, Kirkleski was named to the Lafayette Maroon Club Hall Of Fame. In 2008, he was added to the Nutley High School Athletic Hall of Fame.

Kirkleski, 75, died on May 6, 1980 in Chatham, New Jersey.

Sources: Third Half Club Nutley High School Hall of Fame; Nutley Sun; Ancestry.com. 1910 United States Federal Census [database on-line]. Lehi, UT, USA: Ancestry.com Operations Inc., 2006; Wikipedia contributors. "Frank Kirkleski." Wikipedia, The Free Encyclopedia. Wikipedia, The Free Encyclopedia, 4 Jan. 2017. Web. 24 Jul. 2018; Creative Commons Attribution-ShareAlike License; http://people.famouswhy.com/frank_kirkleski/; http://www.njsportsheroes.com/frankkirkleskifb.html; http://www.profootballarchives.com.

Angelo Pucci

Sports promoter Angelo Pucci was born on April 7, 1907, in Nutley, NJ.

He had one year of high school. In 1935 and 1940, with his wife Antoinette and son Nicholas, he rented at 8 Witherspoon Street, Nutley. Following the loss of his wife, in 1946, he married her sister Virginia. In 1948 he moved to 293 Chestnut Street and lived there with his children Geraldine, Dennis and Kenneth. He later lived on Hancox Avenue until his death on January 2, 1979.

Pucci was induced into the New Jersey Boxing Hall of Fame on November 20, 1992. According to NJ Boxing HOF, Pucci was the only manager to have his fighter headline in Madison Square Garden after being KO'd in four previous fights.

In 1942, Pucci was named one of the Top 10 Best Dressed Men in America.

Pucci managed Rocky Marciano's first 28 fights in Providence, Rhode Island and Boston. Among others, Pucci managed these boxers: Tippy Larkin, Mickey Greb, Roscoe Manning, Frankie Cann, Frankie Duane, Mike Piskin, Wallace Cross, Mickey Bottone, Charlie Smith, Benny Williams, George Aravio, Lloyd Marshall, Steve Osca, and Al Marrone.

Sources: Ancestry.com. 1940 United States Federal Census [database on-line]. Provo, UT, USA: Ancestry.com Operations, Inc., 2012; Ancestry.com. U.S. City Directories, 1822-1995 [database on-line]. Provo, UT, USA: Ancestry.com Operations, Inc., 2011; http://www.njboxinghof.org/angelo-pucci/.

Raymond E. Blum

American speed skater Raymond Edward "Ray" Blum was born in on April 11, 1919, in Nutley, NJ. He lived with his parents Joseph and Ella, and his brother Joseph, and sister Helen at 12 Evelyn Place.

Blum graduated Nutley High School in the Class of 1937. He was inducted into the Third Half Club Nutley High School Hall of Fame in 1997.

He competed at the 1948 Winter Olympics in St. Moritz, Switzerland. He placed 20th in the Men's 1500 metres competition in a field of 45, and 17th in the Men's 5000 metres event in a field of 40.

Blum was a member of the Paterson Skating Club. He enlisted in the U.S. Navy on Sept. 6, 1944 and was discharged on June 5, 1946.

Following his service during WWII, he attended the Newark College of Engineering at the New Jersey Institute of Technology and earned a Bachelor's degree 1950. Blum was an electrical engineer for many aerospace companies including Kearfott Guidance and Navigation, and Collsman Instrument. He was an engineer for the guidance system for the Apollo I moon shot.

On May 17, 1969, Blum was inducted into the American National Speed Skating Museum and Hall of Fame. On October 26, 1996, Blum was inducted into the NJIT Highlanders' Hall of Fame for his success as both a cyclist and a speed skater.

Blum, 91, died May 10, 2010, in Little Falls, NJ. He was survived by his wife, the former Louise M. Voorhis.

Sources: Third Half Club Nutley High School Hall of Fame; Wikipedia contributors. "Ray Blum." Wikipedia, The Free Encyclopedia. Wikipedia, The Free Encyclopedia, 28 Mar. 2018. Web. 24 Jul. 2018; https://www.bizub.com/obituary/Raymond-Edward-Blum/Little-Falls-NJ/782813; Ancestry.com. 1920 United States Federal Census [database on-line]. Provo, UT, USA: Ancestry.com Operations, Inc., 2010. Images reproduced by FamilySearch; Ancestry.com. 1930 United States Federal Census [database on-line]. Provo, UT, USA: Ancestry.com Operations Inc., 2002; Ancestry.com. U.S., Department of Veterans Affairs BIRLS Death File, 1850-2010 [database on-line]. Provo, UT, USA: Ancestry.com Operations, Inc., 2011.

Clifford Mapes

New York Yankees outfielder Clifford Franklin Mapes (March 13, 1922 – December 5, 1996) lived with his wife Betty at 215 Coeyman Avenue, Nutley, NJ.

Mapes played five seasons of Major League Baseball as an outfielder for the New York Yankees, St. Louis Browns and Detroit Tigers.

He played for the New York Yankees from 1948 to 1951. Mapes wore number 3 for the Yankees until that number was retired in honor of Babe Ruth. Mapes then wore number 13 before switching to number 7. When Mapes was traded by the Yankees in 1951, Mickey Mantle took uniform number 7. Mapes, thus, is mainly remembered as the Yankee who wore both Babe Ruth's and Mickey Mantle's numbers.

Born on March 13, 1922, in Sutherland, Neb., Mapes, 74, died on December 5, 1996, in Pryor, Okla.

Sources: 1950 Nutley Alphabetical Directory; 1952 Nutley Alphabetical Directory; Wikipedia contributors. "Cliff Mapes." Wikipedia, The Free Encyclopedia. Wikipedia, The Free Encyclopedia, 26 Mar. 2018. Web. 24 Jul. 2018.

Gilbert McDougald

New York Yankees ballplayer Gilbert James "Gil" McDougald lived with his wife Lucille and family at 94 Mapes Avenue, Nutley, NJ. He owned and operated Yankee Building Maintenance at 324 Passaic Avenue.

Martha Stewart's first brush with fame came in 1961, according to youdontknowjersey.com. She became the occasional babysitter for the children of Mickey Mantle, Yogi Berra, and McDougald of the New York Yankees. The Mantles had four boys, all under the age of ten and Merlyn Mantle was overwhelmed. Martha would organize birthday parties and babysit for all four. "They would behave for Martha," declared Martha, and her domestic career thus began.

McDougald spent ten seasons as a Yankees infielder from 1951 to 1960. He led all American League infielders in double plays at three different positions – at third base in 1952, at second base in 1955 and shortstop in 1957.

McDougald was a member of eight American League pennant winners and five World Series Champions. He was also the American League Rookie of the Year in 1951 and a five-time All-Star. He was known for accidentally hitting a line drive that severely injured Herb Score's right eye in 1957.

His last appearance was in Game Seven of the 1960 World Series against the Pittsburgh Pirates; as a pinch runner in the top of the ninth, he scored on Yogi Berra's ground ball to tie the game at 9–9. The Pirates, however, won the Series.

In 1958, McDougald was given the Lou Gehrig Memorial Award, which is awarded annually by the Phi Delta Theta fraternity (to which Gehrig belonged) at Columbia University. He retired in 1960 at age 32.

McDougald was born on May 19, 1928, and died of prostate cancer on November 28, 2010.

Sources: Anthony Iannarone; Nutley Alphabetical Directory 1952, 1954, 1956, 1958; Yogi Berra, Eternal Yankee, by Allen Barra, W.W. Norton & Co.; youdontknowjersey.com; Wikipedia contributors. "Gil McDougald." Wikipedia, The Free Encyclopedia. Wikipedia, The Free Encyclopedia, 23 Jul. 2018. Web. 24 Jul. 2018.

William Skowron

New York Yankees ballplayer William Joseph Skowron owned and operated R & S Trophy Corp., at 310 Washington Avenue, Nutley, NJ. Nicknamed "Moose", he was an American professional baseball first baseman for 13 seasons from 1954 to 1967.

Moose made his Major League debut April 13, 1954, for the New York Yankees. He played in eight All-Star games and on five World Series champion teams, 1956, 1958, 1961, 1962, and 1963.

In 1962, the Yankees traded him to the Los Angeles Dodgers. He played his last Major League Baseball game with the California Angels on October 1, 1967. He played in a total of 1,478 major-league games, all but 15 as a first baseman. He was in 13 games as a third baseman and two as a second baseman.

Born on December 18, 1930, in Chicago, Skowron, 81, died on April 27, 2012, in Arlington Heights, Ill.

Sources: Wikipedia contributors. "Bill Skowron." Wikipedia, The Free Encyclopedia. Wikipedia, The Free Encyclopedia, 23 Jul. 2018. Web. 24 Jul. 2018.

Ollan Cassell

Nutley's Olympic track and field runner Ollan Cassell used to run and train in Boys Park and Yanticaw Park. An outstanding runner in high school and college, Cassell was an American sprinter in the 1950s and 1960s.

Representing the United States at the 1964 Olympics in Tokyo, he took the gold medal in the men's 4×400 meter relay.

Cassell's most ardent supporter has been his wife, the former Cathy Aires of Nutley, N J. They met at University of Houston, in Houston, Texas. There he took up the quarter-mile.

Cassell won his first AAU championship title in 1957 in 200 meter. In 1962, he won gold medals in the 400 meter and 4×400 meter relay and a silver medal in the 4×100 meter relay at the World Military Championships. The following year, at the 1963 Pan American Games, Cassell won two gold medals in the relays and was second in 200 meter and sixth in 100 meter races.

In his early 30s, he became the executive director of the Amateur Athletic Union.

All six of their children – Chris, Cindy, Colleen, Colette, Craig and Curt – participated in sports, and four competed at the college level.

He was born Ollan Castle, with seven brothers and a sister. Along the way, some newspaper accounts listed his last name as Cassell. He changed it legally in 1961 at the urging of the Army when he was commissioned as a lieutenant after graduation at Houston.

Cassell was born on October 5, 1936, in Nickelsville, Va. He graduated from Appalachia High School in Appalachia, Va. In 2006, he was elected to the United States National Track and Field Hall of Fame as a contributor.

Sources: Wikipedia contributors. "Ollan Cassell." Wikipedia, The Free Encyclopedia. Wikipedia, The Free Encyclopedia, 28 Mar. 2018. Web. 24 Jul. 2018; Ron Coeyman; Joseph Giambanco; Bill Lane, http://www.timesnews.net/Sports/2010/07/04/Memory-Lane-Ollan-Cassell-has-attended-every-Olympic-Games-since-1964-either-as-athlete-or-track-and-field-representative'.

Ken Nicosia

Nutley High School Class of 1975 grad Ken Nicosia turned his love of skiing into a career and created an opportunity to improve ski equipment along the way.

Nicosia always loved to race and ski fast, so after a turn at Bloomfield College, Bloomfield, NJ., he took to ski-bumming at Snowbird, Utah. While savoring the fresh mountain air, he found a tech rep position with ski equipment maker Trappeur-Spalding-Caber on the Pro Tour and later entered retail management for Sitzmark ski shop in Nutley.

He joined ski boot producer Lange in 1979 as service manager where he focused on the company's racing activities, helping racer chasers, young skiers, in the field. In 1982, Ken Nicosia was promoted to Racing Coordinator. For the next two years, he traveled the world over with the U.S. and Canadian ski teams through the 1984 Sarajevo Olympics in which his Lange boots garnered six gold medals. He brought his ski tuning expertise to the company when Lange USA took over the distribution of Authier skis that would eventually be renamed Lange.

In 1984, Nicosia joined Fischer/Dynafit, developing their new race boot.

Nicosia's photography was used in a ski movie about William Dean "Bill" Johnson, the first American Olympic champion alpine ski racer. Nicosia was featured in films by American ski and snowboarding filmmaker Warren Miller.

Through the years, Nicosia took home gold in the New Jersey Ski Racing Association for slalom and giant slalom and also gold for downhill in the Eastern Region Snowsports Association.

In 2018, Nicosia works in Nutley and still calls New Jersey home, but he's never far from the next ski run.

Sources: Ken Nicosia; http://lange-ski-boots.blogspot.com/1984/04/ken-nicosia.html; https://www.linkedin.com/in/ken-nicosia-b2a22635/; http://www.skinet.com/warrenmiller/a-legacy-will-live-on; *Wikipedia contributors. "List of Warren Miller films." Wikipedia, The Free Encyclopedia. Wikipedia, The Free Encyclopedia, 25 Oct. 2017. Web. 26 Jul. 2018; Wikipedia contributors. "Bill Johnson (skier)." Wikipedia, The Free Encyclopedia. Wikipedia, The Free Encyclopedia, 16 Jul. 2018. Web. 26 Jul. 2018; Wikipedia contributors. "Warren Miller (director)." Wikipedia, The Free Encyclopedia. Wikipedia, The Free Encyclopedia, 10 Jul. 2018. Web. 26 Jul. 2018; Wikipedia contributors. "Lange (ski boots)." Wikipedia, The Free Encyclopedia. Wikipedia, The Free Encyclopedia, 16 Feb. 2018. Web. 26 Jul. 2018.*

Tony Williams

Sportswriter Tony Williams began his education at Washington School and Franklin Middle School. The Nutley High School grad, Class of 1992, played football as a freshman and a senior, as well as basketball in his junior high and freshman years. He graduated Nutley High School in the Class of 1992.

Williams earned a degree at William Paterson University in 1998, and almost immediately began writing for daily newspapers. He worked as a paid intern at the *Herald News*, and moved to the Bergen *Record* that fall.

While at the Record, Williams freelanced for *SLAM Magazine* and helped run a basketball site called *The Basketball Beat*, where he covered some future stars when they were still prep and college players.

He wrote for *The Record* until February 2006, when he joined *Metro New York Newspaper* to cover the Knicks. He's been on the Knicks beat since. He also writes for *Salute Magazine*.

Williams covered the Giants during the final few games of the 2008 season, and continues that beat, along with the Brooklyn Nets, New York Jets, and New York City Football Club. He has covered March Madness, the NBA Playoffs, and Super Bowls.

Williams lived in the same two-bedroom apartment on Passaic Avenue from 1981 to 2003 when he married. "Nutley is still the place I come back to any time I need a pizza fix! And I still consider it my home despite not living there for over 13 years," he says.

Sources: Anthony Williams; Metro, https://www.metro.us/profile/tony-williams; Salute Magazine, https://salutemag.com/author/tonywilliams/; Wikipedia contributors. "New York City FC." Wikipedia, The Free Encyclopedia. Wikipedia, The Free Encyclopedia, 25 Jul. 2018. Web. 26 Jul. 2018.

John Strauch

John "Jack" Strauch played both football and baseball for the Maroon Raiders. He earned five varsity letters.

In baseball, Strauch received All-County recognition, and, All-Metro and Scholastic All-American football honors.

Strauch graduated Nutley High School in the Class of 1961. He was inducted into the Third Half Club Nutley High School Hall of Fame in 1989.

He earned an athletic scholarship to Columbia University in New York, where he earned his undergrad and MBA. At Columbia University, Strauch played football for four years where his gridiron performance earned him All-Ivy recognition.

A natural athlete, he continued to run several 5k's over the years, and taught spinning a few nights a week at Gold's Gym. He retired as CFO at Coastal Corrugated, in North Charleston, S.C.

Born in 1943, Strauch died on May 20, 2015, after a brave battle with leukemia.

Sources: Third Half Club Nutley High School Hall of Fame; Nutley Sun, July 5, 1984; Charleston Post & Courier on May 31, 2015.

Donald Chuy

Donald "Don" Chuy grew up in Nutley, New Jersey, and participated in football and track. He received six varsity letters and was selected All-County, All-Metro and All-State in football.

Chuy graduated Nutley High School in the Class of 1959. He was inducted 1989 into the Third Half Club Nutley High School Hall of Fame in 1989.

Chuy attended Clemson University where he earned a Bachelor of Science degree. For his excellence in football, Chuy was All-ACC and received honorable mention All-American. He also played in the East-West Shrine game and was on the All-Star team that defeated Lombardi's Packers.

After college, Chuy he was pick 67 in round five of the 1963 NFL draft, and pick 38 in round five of the AFL draft. He was signed by the Los Angeles Rams and that season was named NFL Rookie of the Year.

While playing for the Rams in 1965, he and several of his teammates played cameo roles as football players in the Perry Mason episode, "The Case of the 12th Wildcat."

Chuy, 72, died on January 6, 2014, in Myrtle Beach, S.C.

Sources: Third Half Club Nutley High School Hall of Fame; Nutley Sun, July 5, 1984, January 26, 1989; Wikipedia contributors. "Don Chuy." Wikipedia, The Free Encyclopedia. Wikipedia, The Free Encyclopedia, 9 Nov. 2017. Web. 26 Jul. 2018.

William Vonroth

William "Billy" Vonroth was a gifted, determined student-athlete in every sense. Although he was star on the playing fields, more importantly, he was a star in the classroom. A three-sport athlete, he played football, basketball and baseball. His football talents were substantial.

Vonroth graduated Nutley High School in the Class of 1963. He was inducted 1989 into the Third Half Club Nutley High School Hall of Fame in 2004.

His athleticism and intelligence earned him the starting role as quarterback on the gridiron and carried him to the basketball team and baseball. He was selected as the shortstop for the All Essex County Baseball Team as a Junior and Senior. In addition he was also selected as a senior to an All Baseball State Team as well as being named the American Legion Scholar/Athlete of the year.

Vonroth attended Lafayette College where he continued his academic and baseball careers. His prowess earned him a place in the Lehigh Valley Hall of Fame and he became only the third individual to be honored by the American Legion as a Scholastic and Collegiate Award honoree.

He pursued his education and attended medical school at the University of Medicine and Dentistry of New Jersey, and is a highly respected orthopedic surgeon. Dr. Vonroth's dedication to Nutley athletics remains strong, and he served as Raiders team physician for more than 20 years.

Sources: Third Half Club Nutley High School Hall of Fame; Nutley Sun, July 5, 1984.

Arthur Zinicola

Arthur "Art" Zinicola was involved in baseball, football and wrestling. He earned a total of ten Varsity letters. In wrestling, Zinicola was a two-time

Heavyweight Champion. In baseball, he received All-County, All-Metropolitan and All-State Honors.

At Wagner College, Art again earned ten Varsity letters, and received his degree in Education. He was selected All-MAC and All-Metropolitan in baseball. In wrestling, he was undefeated in his junior year. Zinicola was MVP in wrestling and baseball for two years and voted Outstanding Athlete of his class.

Zinicola graduated Nutley High School in the Class of 1967. He was inducted into the Third Half Club Nutley High School Hall of Fame in 1989.

Sources: Third Half Club Nutley High School Hall of Fame; Nutley Sun, July 5, 1984.

Mel Stottlemyre

A wonderful thing happened on Alexander Avenue in 1968. That's when New York Yankees pitcher Mel Stottlemyre and his family moved next door to *Nutley Sun* publisher Frank Orechio and diagonally across from writer Helen Maguire.

While some of the old-timers today (who were kids in '68) remember Stottlemyre's cookouts in his driveway, Maguire captured the excitement in a column she wrote for the *Sun* in October, at season's end when the celebrity family headed back home to Washington state.

Frank and Edith Orechio introduced the new couple to the neighborhood at an evening cocktail party. Mayor Harry w. Chenoweth showed up, as well as all the grown-ups on the block. Maguire noted that as soon as the invitations went out, there was a sudden dearth of babysitters.

She noted the lines of boys at the Stottlemyre's door, proffering baseballs and seeking autographs and pictures. "This happens every year. It'll stop within the week," predicted the unflappable Stot and it did.

While the pitcher was on his first road trip, Jean Stottlemyre had run out of money and found that despite her name, few in the new town were anxious to cash an out-of-state-check. Maguire also reported that Jean locked herself out of the house, "and it took the combined efforts of the local newspaper publisher and the greatest Yankee fan" on the Alexander Avenue to get her back in. The house-spouse also somehow "turned off the house's hot water supply while looking for the outside outlet and she couldn't remember which valve was which."

By the second road trip, Maguire reported, "Jean had become part of a canasta foursome. The other players soon learned not to schedule a game if Mel was pitching. If he was winning, she was so elated she couldn't concentrate and if he was losing, she was so annoyed, she didn't care.

"When the Yankees were home, the youngsters soon learned to recognize the Thunderbirds that belonged to [fellow Yankees players] Tom Tresh and Jake Gibbs. People watched Yankee games whether they were fans or not just to see how Mel was doing."

Stottlemyre was a five-time All-Star for the New York Yankees during a career from 1964 to 1974 and ranks fifth on the Yankees' all-time list for career wins with 164. A solid-hitting pitcher, Stottlemyre once hit a rare inside-the-park grand slam, and in another game recorded five base hits in five at-bats.

Born on November 13, 1941, in Hazelton, Mo., Stottlemyre grew up in Mabton, Wash. He pitched in American Legion Baseball and attended Mabton High School and Yakima Valley Community College.

A Yankees scout discovered Stottlemyre pitching for Yakima's baseball team, and signed him to a contract with no signing bonus on June 10, 1961.

Called up midseason in 1964, Stottlemyre went 9–3 to help the Yankees to their fifth consecutive pennant while being on the cover of *The Sporting News*. In the 1964 World Series, Stottlemyre faced Bob Gibson of the St. Louis Cardinals three times in the seven-game Series.

Stottlemyre threw 40 shutouts in his 11-season career, the same number as Hall of Fame lefty Sandy Koufax. Two of his sons, Todd and Mel Jr., followed their father by becoming major league pitchers. His other son, Jason, died of leukemia at the age of 11 in 1981.

1968 had been a good year for the families on Alexander Avenue, Maguire wrote, who had gotten to know Mel and Jean, Mel Jr. and Todd. The famous neighbors had become new friends.

In 1973, Maguire wrote, "I inherit clothes, too, mostly from Jean Stottlemyre and what doesn't fit me is passed along to a friend just a little bit more amply endowed. Sometimes, something reaches a third party if neither one of us can wear it but we make a concerted effort to keep whatever we can, believe me."

In 1991, Frank Orechio wrote, "Former New York Yankees pitching star Mel Stottlemyre, and his wife, Jean, make sure they include *Nutley Sun*'s Helen Maguire on their annual Christmas card list." He added, "The Stottlemyres were perfect neighbors."

Sources: Ever Wonder What Happens When a Star Moves Next Door? by Helen Maguire, Nutley Sun, October 31, 1968; Helen's Thing: Clothes, Seasons, Searches by Helen Maguire, Nutley Sun, Sept. 20, 1973; Window on My World, Frank Orechio, Nutley Sun, January 3, 1991; Wikipedia contributors. "Mel Stottlemyre." Wikipedia, The Free Encyclopedia. Wikipedia, The Free Encyclopedia, 26 May. 2018. Web. 27 Jul. 2018.

Sam Stellatella

High school and university football icon Saverio "Sam" F. Stellatella, was born on August 19, 1938, in Nutley, NJ. He graduated Nutley High School in the Class of 1956. He was an original inductee into the Third Half Club Nutley High School Hall of Fame in 1988.

Joseph Rocco Cervasio, author and a long-time friend noted, Stellatella's "legend began on the grassy tundra of the fabled Park Oval in Nutley. There he was named High School All American in football in the mid-fifties as a ferocious linebacker for the Maroon Raiders. Also being named All State in baseball at Nutley High, Sam went on to Penn State where he lettered as a lineman and placekicker. His proud wearing of Number 62 for the Nittany Lions was just the beginning of his life-long loyalty to Linebacker University, their coaches, his teammates, the fans and all things Penn State."

At Nutley High in his junior year, 1954, Stellatella was named to first team All-County, All-Metro and All-State in football, and honored as outstanding player of the year. In 1955, he was First team All-County, All-Metro and All-American, and first team All-State baseball Group 4.

Stellatella lettered in football at Penn State, 1957, 1958, and 1959. He earned his degree in history from Penn State where he was a three-position player in the 1950s, was on the Letterman's Club and won the Liberty Bowl in 1959.

Stellatella played in the inaugural 1959 Liberty Bowl, part of the 1959 football bowl game season, December 19, 1959, at the Philadelphia Municipal Stadium in Philadelphia. The competing teams were the Alabama Crimson Tide headed by Bear Bryant, representing the Southeastern Conference (SEC), and the Penn State Nittany Lions, competing as a football independent. In a game dominated by defenses, Penn State won 7–

0. In a game dominated by both defenses, the only points were scored at the end of the second quarter by the Nittany Lions on a fake field goal. This lone touchdown was scored by Roger Kochman on a 17-yard reception from Galen Hall with Stellatella adding the extra point.

In a *New Jersey Monthly* story, Stellatella, who dated Stewart when she was a senior in high school, said he remembers her as "beautiful and wholesome."

In 2002, Stellatella was named to the New Jersey State Interscholastic Athletic Association Hall of Fame.

Stellatella taught in Belleville, Hillside, and Lyndhurst. He finished his teaching career at Manchester Township High School where he also coached football, noted Kevin Williams of 92.7 WOBM in Ocean County, New Jersey. "Sam used his teacher contacts for a successful second career selling insurance."

Besides growing up in Nutley, Stellatella lived in Bloomfield before moving to Toms River, NJ. Whether he lived near or far, he stayed true to Penn Stated and his hometown. He continued as a member supporting the Nutley Chapter of UNICO National and other local groups.

Stellatella, who proudly served in the U.S. Army, died at age 78 on March 26, 2017, at his Toms River home.

Sources: Sam Stellatella, email, January 10, 2015; Dan Geltrude; Carolyn Stellatella; Third Half Club Nutley High School Hall of Fame; Good New Jersey Monthly, https://njmonthly.com › Jersey Living; Wikipedia contributors. "1959 Liberty Bowl."; Star-Ledger, March 29, 2017; News on the Doorstep, Passing Thoughts from Joseph Rocco Cervasio; http://joecervasio.typepad.com/goodnews/2017/04/sam-stellatella-all-american.html; Wikipedia, The Free Encyclopedia. Wikipedia, The Free Encyclopedia, 28 Jun. 2018;. Web. 24 Jul. 2018; "U.S., School Yearbooks, 1880-2012"; Year: 1954; Sam Stellatella: A Real Character With Cold-Eeze, Kevin Williams, http://wobm.com/sam-stellatella-a-real-character-wth-cold-eeze/; Nutley High School - Exit Yearbook (Nutley, NJ), Class of 1956, Page 99, www.e-yearbook.com.

INDEX

Anderson, Nelle, 8
Armstrong, Estelle Manon, 21
Atzeri, Emmanuel and Jeannine, 83

Balde, Julio, 73
Baldino, Josephine, 25
Berger, Ellen, 16
Berger, Theodore, 71
Biondi, Anthony, 84
Birkby, Noel Phyllis, 42
Blum, Ray, 97
Booth, Thomas H., 75
Brackett, Dr. Elizabeth, 17
Brown, Elizabeth Stow, 7
Brown, Hermanus, 67
Brown, Samuel W., 88
Buset, Linda, 47

Cassell, Ollan, 100
Chiga, Sr. Romilda, 32
Chuy, Don, 105
Ciccone, Elsie, 37
Clark, Bertha, 38
Clendinning, Jeanette, 7
Cooper, Laurie, 50
Craine, Marilyn, 40
Culari, Nick, 85

Danachek, Catherine, 27
De St. Clement, Dorothea, 14
DiFrancesco, David, 58
Donadio, Joyce, 24
Drewes, George and Alma, 81
Dwyer, Daniel, 79

Eldridge, Dorothy Daggett, 17
Elder, Arthur, 52

Fenske, Rev. Jill, 41
Ferrara, Gail, 50
Ferraro, Bernadette, 40
Ferraro, Gerald, 70
Fikus, Vivian, 19
Fleitell, Michelle, 31
Florence, Lella Secor, 12
Florence, Mary Sargant, 13
Furnari, Susan, 49

Galloway, Wendy, 50
Gilbert, David, 59
Goodson, Sally, 45
Greulich, Nancy, 28
Guenzler, Gertrude, 5

Hall, Norma, 18
Hall Sharp, Royance, 57
Hoffer, Maxine, 31
Hunt, Larry, 64
Hutchinson, Edith, 35

Jaret, Keith, 90

Keenan, Ruth, 21
Kinsley, Elvira, 9
Kirkleski, Frank, 94
Kramer, Dick, 60

La Monte, George, 81
Lenson, Barry, 63
Lester, Alice, 23
Lovell, Tom, 53
Lynch, Alice, 29

Magee, Abbie, 16
Mapes, Clifford, 98
Marion, Maureen, 33
Marsh, Anne Steele, 19
McDougald, Gilbert, 98
Miller, Louise, 20

Mountsier, Margaret, 26

Negra, August, 74
Nicosia, Ken, 102
Nunzio, Charles, 54

O'Connell Milton, 94

Palladino, Ottavio, 86
Peddieson, Dorinda, 10
Pène du Bois, William, 56
Perrotta, Mary, 39
Petracco, Franca, 44
Perry, Beatrice, 5
Pontoriero, Giacomo, 89
Powers, Ada Weigel, 18
Priolo, Mel, 47
Proal, Emma Jane, 10
Pucci, Angelo, 96

Rotonda, Anne, 34
Rubino, Dominick, 76
Rubino Ryder, Mary, 46
Rummel, Peggy, 30
Rutan, Florence, 36

Sandford, Olive, 13
Scheckel, Rosalie, 36
Seymour, Grace, 15
Shannon, Frances, 45
Skowron, William, 100
Stellatella, Sam, 110
Stone, Ellery, 69
Stottlemyre, Mel, 107

Tangorra, Frank, 71
Taylor, Allen Robert, 87
Taylor, Keith, 91

Volpe, Michael, aka Clams
Casino, 65
Vonroth, William, 106

Walcott Morgan, Faith, 11
Williams, Tony, 103
Wilson, David, 77

Yorton, Elise, 22

Zinicola, Art, 107

NUTLEY NOTABLES Volume One

Carolyn and Rich Agresta adopted retired racing greyhounds. The greyhound adoption process is simple, but thorough, with prospective adopters vetted through their veterinarian or personal contacts.

Dorothy Allison earned a national reputation for helping many people by using her psychic ability. She also assisted in several well-known cases including the Son of Sam murders, and the John Wayne Gacy cases.

Anthony "Andy" Andriola spent decades travelling from school to school sharing many tales of action in North Africa, Sicily, England, France, Belgium and Germany.

Keith Banks began his career in 1981 at Home Insurance. In 1984, he joined JP Morgan as an equity research analyst. In 1988, he took on the role of portfolio manager. In 1996, Banks was promoted to head of U.S. equity.

Anthony Baratta Jr., is one of America's foremost leaders of interior designs.

John Barbata is a world-class musician, a drummer, whose extraordinary life began at the age of three, when he met Albert Einstein, to the present.

Phelan Beale was married to Edith Ewing Bouvier Beale, an American socialite and amateur singer, known for her eccentric lifestyle.

Ruth Bedford dedicated her life toward supporting local and statewide community organizations, including the Nutley Family Services Bureau, Nutley Senior Citizens Housing, and the Republican Club of Nutley.

Judge Stanley Bedford was appointed to the NJ District Court by Gov. William Cahill in 1971. Over the years, Judge Bedford volunteered his legal expertise to Nutley charitable groups including the Red Cross chapter.

Cathleen Benko is vice chairman and managing principal, Deloitte LLP. Benko is a self-made woman who distinguished herself in the Global Business World. She was named a "Frontline Leader".

Rita and William Berg lived on Nutley Avenue for more than 30 years. Berg left a great sum of money "to preserve a bit of clean country midst a built-up town." Nutley used the sum for improvements to the park.

Julian Bigelow obtained a master's degree at the Massachusetts Institute of Technology. During World War II, he assisted Norbert Wiener's research on automated fire control for anti-aircraft guns.

Julian 'Bud' Blake achieved world-wide recognition as the award-winning creator of the syndicated "Tiger" comic strip.

Actor Robert Blake was born Michael James Vincenzo Gubitosi in 1933, in Nutley, NJ. He began his film career as one of the Little Rascals, but is perhaps best known for playing Baretta on TV.

Carol Blazejowski served as senior vice president and general manager of the New York Liberty basketball team. She is one of the top players in the history of women's basketball.

Abram Blum was Nutley's first mayor under the commission form of government adopted in 1912. Blum, Richard W. Booth, and others organized the Yantacaw Volunteer Fire Department.

Philip M. Boffey, an editorial board member at The New York Times, was a member of two reporting teams that won Pulitzer Prizes.

Town worker Lucio Bolcato, 51, died in July 1975, of a heart attack during a courageous attempt to rescue two young boys in storm-swollen waters of the Third River.

Enoch Booth was wounded in the Civil War, participating in battles in the Petersburg, Va., area, and never fully recovered, passing away in 1879.

Richard W. Booth was first elected to the school board in 1896, and served as president for 18 years. His foresight is responsible for much of the success of Nutley's schools.

Edith Ewing Bouvier Beale was an American socialite and amateur singer. She was a sister of John "Black Jack" Bouvier, the father of Jacqueline Bouvier Kennedy Onassis and Lee Radziwill.

John. V. Bouvier served as a member of the Nutley Board of Education from 1901 to 1904, and as president of the Yountakah Country Club. He organized the Nutley Gun Club. He was a trial lawyer in New York.

John Bradbury built a stone house on a knoll south of Kingsland's Lane.

This house is what we know today as the Van Riper House.

Larry Brancaccio is a champion motorcycle rider, and 1975 Nutley High School graduate. He became the AHDRA (All Harley Drag Racing Association) Pro Dragster Eastern and World Champion.

Mike Bronco has worked as a mechanic with Ralph Scognamillo at his service station on Bloomfield Avenue and lately at J & R Towne Auto to Centre Street and Union Avenue.

Nutley-based author Anthony Buccino published more than 20 books including four essay collections and three military history books.

Jonathan Budine is a director, designer and editor. In 2002, he was tapped as one of the editors for Michael Moore's Academy Award winning film "Bowling for Columbine".

Henry Cuyler Bunner was an American novelist and poet. The editor of Puck the satire magazine is credited with bringing Mark Twain to The Enclosure and introducing the writer to ice cream at Guthrie's General Store.

Nutley High School Class of 1971 graduate Barbara A. Buono was the Democratic nominee for Governor of New Jersey in the 2013 election. Buono served in the New Jersey Senate from 2002 to 2014.

Jane Grey Burgio was the first woman to become New Jersey Secretary of State. Burgio was appointed by Governor Thomas Kean and served from 1982 to 1990.

Henri Gaston Busignes was working for ITT's Paris Labs on radio direction finders, airplane radio navigation and early radar equipment. With the fall of Paris to Hitler, in 1940, he escaped to the U.S.

Frank Butler was married to sharp-shooter Annie Oakley. Their visits to the Eaton Stone Circus quarters here brought her through town on a train where it's said they fell in love with Nutley.

Janet and Stephen Canonico adopted retired racing greyhounds. The greyhound adoption process is simple, but thorough, with prospective adopters vetted through their veterinarian or personal contacts.

James Carlin, an internationally acclaimed Nutley artist, was a master in the watercolor medium. He won many prestigious prizes, including the George A. Zabriskie Award.

Donna Castellano's long professional acting career includes TV, film, theatre, musical theatre and cabaret, plus commercials from New York to Maryland and Japan.

Loretta Catena and Joseph DelGrosso adopted retired racing greyhounds. The greyhound adoption process is simple, but thorough, with prospective adopters vetted through their veterinarian or personal contacts.

Joseph Cervasio is author of two books. *Bad News On The Doorstep* recalls the infamous 'Mud Bowl' between Nutley and Belleville in the 1960s and captures the flavor of life in Northeast New Jersey.

Tina M. Cervasio, a 1992 NHS graduate, is an Emmy-nominated New York Knicks reporter on the MSG Network. Cervasio's first job out of college was as the Sports Editor for the *Nutley Sun* and *Belleville Times*.

Vicky Chalk is well known for her weekly column, Over The Back Fence, in the *Nutley Sun*, which she has written since 1996. Her positive local columns earned accolades from the New Jersey Press Association.

Paul Chapman, WPA artist, painted the mural of Annie Oakley in the Nutley Post Office.

Harry Chenoweth's dedication to community activities has been recognized as evidenced by his election to the office of mayor for 20 consecutive years.

Port Authority police officer Lt. Robert Cirri rushed to help at the burning towers on September 11. His remains were recovered four other officers and a woman they had been trying to carry out in a rescue chair.

Joanne Cocchiola ran for commissioner in 2004 seeking her father's vacated seat. She not only won, but tallied the most votes of all candidates and was named mayor.

Frank Cocchiola served as a town commissioners for 28 years and on the school board for six years. He oversaw the development of park facilities on Park Avenue and River Road.

Tuskegee Airman Victor Connell was graduated from Class 45-D-SE, on June 27, 1945, having been inducted from Davenport, Iowa

Crossing guard Filomena Coppola was killed on Nov. 4, 1997, sacrificing her life for the children who were walking in the path of a drunk driver.

Capt. Angelica Vitillo Costa served as deputy director of the Navy Nurse Corps from 1966 to 1970. She volunteered for active military duty in 1942, and served in the US Navy Nurse Corps for the next 28 years.

Dr. Angela Christiano is an associate professor at Columbia University whose major focus of research is in the study of inherited skin and hair disorders in humans.

Nutley resident Phil Cuzzi joined the baseball Major League umpire staff in 1999. Since 2000, he has worked throughout both major leagues.

Michael W. Debany served as Commanding Officer of "Camp Nutley" a U.S. Army antiaircraft gun base in town.

Msgr. Anthony DiLuca served as pastor of Holy Family Church from 1933 until his retirement in 1968. During his 35-year tenure, he raised funds to build two church buildings, a school, convent and youth center.

Anthony Theodore De Muro began his political career in Nutley on the Board of Commissioners in 1932. He served until 1964.

Jessica Denay is a single mom of Gabriel, and the author of The Hot Mom's Handbook series, and is regarded as a leading 'mom' expert.

Nicholas L. DePace attended Washington School where his sixth grade teacher, John Walker, introduced him to medicine and encouraged him to pursue his dream of becoming a doctor.

Nutley school crossing guard James DeZarlo was killed when he was struck by a car on Harrison Street at Brookline Avenue on Dec. 14, 1964.

Lt. David Dinan III, was killed March 17, 1969, in Laos, Southeast Asia, after he was forced to bail out of a F105 jet that had been hit by ground fire.

Jane Doyle is the daughter of Bessie Jane Nichols who is a descendant of Thomas Nichols, Sr., who emigrated from England and started the

Nichols Hat Factory which led to Nichols Park.

Gary T. Erbe is a self-taught oil painter. The Enclosure artist's Trompe L'Oeil paintings can be found in many public and private collections throughout the world.

Ken Eulo is the author of 13 novels, five of which were national bestsellers and sold more than 13 million copies.

William Falduti was awarded the Silver Star for his actions serving 82nd Airborne 505 Parachute Infantry Regiment delivering mortar shells to frozen Allied outposts at Bastogne, Belgium.

Steve Fastook, an Emmy award winning television engineer and producer, is senior vice president of technical and commercial operations at CNBC. As a volunteer for OBC-TV during his youth.

Kathryn Beliveau Feuer, a Russian literature scholar lived in Charlottesville, where she was a professor at the University of Virginia.

Frank Fowler was an American figure and portrait painter. In the late 1890s, he resided in a home on at 16 The Enclosure Artists Colony. He built a large studio on the back of that house, where he painted.

Pasquale DeFrancesco used the name Joseph to join the U.S. Navy. According to his family, 'Joe' was on a ship that was sunk and he spent time in the water where he developed pneumonia and died on Jan. 19, 1918.

'Pat' Francisco served in WWII and was wounded in the European Theatre. He had been left for dead by the Germans during the Normandy Invasion. He was named after his older brother who died in WWI.

Fine photography artist Thomas Francisco was raised in Nutley where he attended Holy Family School and was graduated from Nutley High School. His creative career spans over 38 years.

Ronald Fraser, nicknamed "The Wizard of College Baseball," never had a losing season in 30 years as head coach at the University of Miami.

Bevan M. French joined the NASA Goddard Space Flight Center, as a planetary geologist and began research on terrestrial meteorite impact craters.

Fred M. Frobose had a dance studio at 24 Erie Place where he taught most of Nutley how to dance including Martha Stewart. She referred to him on her television show as "Our Local Fred Astaire".

Johann Friedrich "Fritz" Frobose arrived from Bremen, Germany, on Sept. 4, 1854. He married Christiana Usaner and later moved to their Nutley home overlooking the Mud Hole.

Mike Frobose is a trustee at Vincent Church and the cemetery is his responsibility. In 2014 Mike was selected as the Nutley Irish Member of the Year and also became a board member of the Nutley Historical Society.

Author and historian, Michael C. Gabriele joined the *Nutley Sun* in 1976. He published The Golden Age of Bicycle Racing in New Jersey and The History of Diners in New Jersey.

Mike Geltrude became the first Nutley High School graduate to receive a varsity letter in collegiate soccer. As a coach and pioneer of Nutley's youth traveling soccer program.

Raquel George began writing novels in her early teens. Her published novels include *Jill/Until Proven Innocent* and *Seventeen Days*.

NHS graduate Paul Goldberger, The New York Times' chief cultural correspondent won a Pulitzer Prize for his architectural criticism.

Hollywood screenwriter Frances Goodrich grew up in Nutley, won the Pulitzer Prize for co-writing the play "Diary of Anne Frank," with her husband Albert Hackett, and wrote classic film screenplays.

Lloyd Goodrich began writing about the arts and became a preeminent Americanist art historian. He served as director of the Whitney Museum of American Art, and a leading author and advocate of American art.

Mary Anne Griese is a certified Yoga teacher and has been introducing people to Yoga for three decades, teaching in Nutley Parks and Rec., Nutley Adult School, and elsewhere.

Bryan Haczyk played American professional ice hockey. Haczyk attended Seton Hall Prep where he won two state championships and won the Gordon Conference MVP award.

Benjamin Hawkins, "The Hawk" began his ascent to professional football fame as a wide receiver and defensive end at Arizona State University.

Dr. Christine E. Haycock pioneered the path for women in the military, especially in medicine, by becoming, in 1952, the Army's first woman intern at the Walter Reed Army Medical Center.

Barbara Hirsch, whose volunteer work in the community began while still a youngster about to enter high school, received Nutley's 2013 Dr. Virginius D. Mattia Public Service Award.

Michael Hirsch is the preeminent authority on the Triangle Shirtwaist Factory Fire, co-produced, researched, and wrote the HBO documentary: "Triangle: Remembering the Fire."

Faith Shapiro Hochberg was named U.S. Attorney for the District of New Jersey.

Arthur Hoeber was a U.S. painter best known for his writing on art-related subjects. He was art director for The New York Times for three years and was assistant editor of the Illustrated American for one year.

John Holland joined the Nutley Police Department in 1972. He attained the rank of sergeant in 1977, captain in 1986, and deputy chief in 1990. He served as Nutley Police Chief from 2006 to 2013.

Victor Morice Hopkins competed from 1921 to 1934, ten years professionally. He represented the U.S. in the 1924 Olympics in Paris as America's number one road racer.

John Lloyd Huck joined Merck & Co., in 1958. He was elected vice president for marketing planning in January 1966, and subsequently president and chief operating officer and chairman of the board in 1985.

Anthony J. Iannarone joined Hoffmann LaRoche where he rapidly developed expertise in the regulation of vitamins and dietary foods. He has been contributing to the Nutley community for more than four decades.

Thomas P. Infusino served as Chairman and CEO of Wakefern Food Corp.

Dr. Richard J. Jackson received the Presidential Distinguished Executive Award from President George W. Bush for his outstanding leadership and extraordinary achievement in service to the nation.

Brigadier General John R. Jannarone commanded a Combat Engineer Battalion and later was promoted to Assistant Engineer of the Eighth Army in New Guinea, the Philippines and Japan.

Maureen Jaret decided she'd help out long-time customer Dennis Paserchia by donating one of her kidneys. The National Kidney Registry found a match through "paired exchange."

Tuskegee airman Edward Jenkins was graduated in Class 45-A-SE on March 11, 1945, having been inducted from Nutley, NJ.

William J. Jernick joined Thomas A. Edison, in Belleville, and rose to Assistant to the Vice President and General Manager. He served as Nutley's Director of Revenue and Finance, and Director of Public Safety.

William Jernick III continued his family's dedication to Nutley serving as president of the Rotary Club and like his father, as Exalted Ruler of the Nutley Elks Lodge.

John F. Kane, former commander of Veterans of Foreign Wars Stuart E. Edgar Post 493 in Nutley, was named State Commander at the VFW convention in 2014. He was named him 2014 Veteran of the Year.

John V. Kelly was a state legislator, banker, Nutley commissioner, mayor, and humanitarian. From 1988 to 1992, he served as Nutley mayor and headed the Public Safety Department through May 1996.

Joseph Kingsland purchased about 40 acres of land at a Sheriff's sale on Nov. 22, 1790, for eleven pounds, five shillings.

Dorota Kopiczko, 26, an accountant at Marsh & McLennan, worked on the 100th floor of the World Trade Center's Tower 1, where she perished on September 11.

Journalist Robert Ellis Kur gained attention in the mid-1990s for his coverage of the lawsuits against the tobacco industries. He later became an anchor for MSNBC and was later the White House correspondent.

Anthony 'Barry' LaForgia launched "Southwest Medical Teams," linking people in need with teams of volunteers, beginning in Mexico, Jamaica and Armenia, and later expanding to 65 countries.

Port Authority engineer Franco Lalama perished on September 11, after he cleared everyone out of the engineering office on the 64th floor of 1 World Trade Center, then turned back to make sure no one was left behind.

William Lambert was key in shaping the layout of many Nutley neighborhoods and much of the town's character including the establishment of the memorial park.

In 1947, Amuel E. Lardier opened Lardier Pharmacy at 115 Franklin Avenue, Nutley. Lardier Pharmacy operated at the same location until its sale in 1986. Lardier continued to work in local pharmacies until age 92.

Edward C. Lauber started Lauber Imports in his mom's basement on Grant Street in 1980. With his son Mark E. Lauber, they built the fine wine wholesaler into one of the most highly regarded companies in the industry.

Senator Frank R. Lautenberg was elected to the U.S. Senate in 1982. After a brief retirement, he won a fourth term in 2002 and was re-elected to a fifth term in 2008. He graduated Nutley High School in 1941.

Capt. Rita Lenihan, USN, of Nutley, was appointed Director of the WAVES and Assistant Chief of Naval Personnel for Women on Sept. 1, 1966. Captain Lenihan was commissioned an Ensign in June 1943.

Artist Michael Lenson bought his 'dream studio' at 16 Enclosure Artists Colony and raised his family there. He headed the NJ WPA mural projects and painted murals in Newark City Hall and elsewhere.

Starks Lewis is best known for one of the two giant United States flags he's rigged to a giant tree in front of his house since 2002.

Vincent LoCurcio and partner Thomas Infusino joined Wakefern and together operated the Nutley Park ShopRite. The partnership continues today with LoCurcio's son, Vincent LoCurcio III.

Flora Louden was an active member of the Rotary Club Auxiliary, the Nutley Girl Scout Council, the Tri-Town Business and Professional Women's Association of Nutley.

John Lucy marked his 35th year of service to Nutley's board of commissioners in 1978, the year he was honored with the Dr. Virginius Dante Mattia Community Service Award.

Diane and Mario Mandour owned and operated Santini Bros. Pizzeria and Restaurant from 1989 to 2014. Diane and Mario met while both worked at the at the Gondola Restaurant on Franklin Avenue.

WWII veteran, Daniel Marese returned to his hometown of Nutley and for more than 50 years assisted, started and succeeded in a variety of community accomplishments.

Malcolm Marmorstein was the head writer for all 82 episodes of "The Doctors" soap opera on TV. When that show ended he moved to "Dark Shadows" where he worked on more than 80 episodes.

Reginald Marsh was born in 1898. Two years later, his father, Fred Dana Marsh, moved to 16 The Enclosure Artists Colony. Reginald was taught to draw, influenced not only by his father.

Donna Martin worked at the Dept. of Defense Inspector General investigating whistleblower reprisal allegations.

Virginius D. Mattia, M.D., served as president and CEO of Hoffmann-LaRoche. Dr. Mattia's talents and leadership abilities became manifest through his meteoric advancement.

Bernard "Bus" McGinnity ran a speak-easy in the basement of the Kingsland Manor during Prohibition.

Evan Megaro is a world-renown classical pianist. The 1999 graduate of Nutley High School, played trumpet, French horn, and percussion in the Nutley Marching Band, Nutley Orchestra, and Jazz Ensemble.

Arnold Merritt started his career with the TV series "The Other Face of Goodness". He appeared in the Broadway production of the Archibald McLeish play "JB" with Pat Hingle and John Cassavetes.

Patrick Mirucki, president of VK Media & Internet Services, makes the magic happen behind the scenes. Mirucki became general manager for OBC-TV, a commercial/public access channel in Nutley.

Catherine Murray began her community activities at the age of 14 in 1919, as a Sunday school teacher. She became a Red Cross first aider in 1943.

Richard Nanes is an internationally acclaimed composer and pianist and the recipient of eight consecutive Silver International Angel Awards. He graduated from Nutley High School.

Angelo Nardone operated The Villa Capri, an art salon which had served as a coffeehouse serving local beatniks and bohemians. Nardone's emporium was considered either a work of art or an eyesore.

Grammy Award winning soprano Susan Narucki earned international acclaim as a singer of luminous tone, superb musicianship and distinctive artistry.

Thomas Nichols, Sr., emigrated from England and was married to Mary Hammell. Nichols started a Nichols Hat Factory in Newark and relocated it to Nutley.

William Nolze was posthumously awarded the Silver Star during the Korean War when he distinguished himself by remaining to establish a base of covering fire while his comrades fell back against.

Annie Oakley once wrote that she loved America and Nutley best of all. She and her husband, Frank Butler, lived 304 Grant Avenue.

Carmen Orechio was first elected a member of the Nutley Board of Commissioners in 1968. During his 40 year tenure as a commissioner, he headed the public safety department for 28 years.

Frank A. Orechio purchased the *Nutley Sun* in 1958. He later acquired *Bloomfield Life*, *Belleville Times* and *Glen Ridge Voice* and for what become known as Orechio Communications and included OBC-TV.

The Reverend Monsignor James J. Owens was assigned to Saint Mary's Parish and from October 1922 to September 1965, Saint Mary's grew, adding the rectory, convent, church, school, and an auditorium-gymnasium.

Ron Owens, a music teacher at Nutley schools, cites his most important achievement in Nutley as his work with "Sing-Out, Nutley!" part of the national "Up With People!" movement.

American jazz singer and guitarist Jackie Paris was born Carlo Jackie Paris to Rose and Carlo Paris on Sept. 20, 1926, in Nutley, NJ. As a vocalist, Paris toured with Charlie Parker.

Dennis Paserchia needed a kidney match. When Maureen Jaret heard, she decided she'd help by donating one of her kidneys. The National Kidney Registry matched a "paired exchange."

Narendra "Nick" Patel has owned and operated Fred's Party Shop since 1987. He's seen generations of children from nearby Lincoln School stop in for their snacks. His partner Jitendra "Jay" Patel works the early shift.

Humble barber Mario Pavone supported the Order Sons of Italy orphanage in Nutley. He assisted refugees, collected funds for earthquake victims, Red Cross, the Elks, Special Young Adults, and the Lions Club.

Capt. James W. Pearson downed his first enemy plane on May 30, 1918. He received credit for two more German fighters in June and July, and his two victories in August qualified him as an "ace."

Dr. Andrew L. Pecora, chairman and director of the Cancer Unit at Hackensack University Medical Center, is also the senior scientist for biomedical research at the Hackensack center.

Choreographer Stephen Petronio has been awarded choreography fellowships from the National Endowment for the Arts, and company grants from the NEA and the New York State Council on the Arts.

Eileen L. Poiani, Ph.D., is a third generation Nutleyite on her maternal side. Dr. Poiani's career at Saint Peter's University spanned from being the first woman to teach mathematics to serving as assistant to five presidents.

Steve Politi is a sports columnist for The Star-Ledger in Newark, NJ. Politi, was twice named as one of the top 10 top columnists in the U.S. by the Associated Press.

Cardiologist Eric N. Prystowsky achieved international prominence in teaching, research, and patient care in cardiac electrophysiology.

Milton Prystowsky opened his practice for pediatric cardiology in 1951. He opened the Division of Pediatric Cardiology at the University of Medicine and Dentistry of New Jersey.

Ann Rabinowitz, a former president and school board member, authored two young adult novels, *Knight on Horseback* and *Bethie*.

Paul Radcliffe came to Nutley in 1920, Radcliffe spent nearly $2 million on school buildings doubling student capacity for the growing town..

Lee Radziwill is the daughter of John "Black Jack" Bouvier, and the sister of Jacqueline Bouvier Kennedy Onassis.

Earl Reeder was an organic chemist at Hoffmann-La Roche for 33 years and the co-inventor of the tranquilizer Valium.

Walter F. Reinheimer was elected to the school board in 1927, and was a member when additions were added to Yantacaw and Lincoln schools.

Rev. Lawrence Curtis Roberts became the first black gospel record company producer in the United States. His efforts enabled Savoy Record Company to become a totally gospel label.

Seaman Pervis Robison Jr. was one of 129 servicemen killed on April 10, 1963, when U.S.S. Thresher, a new class of submarine sank during sea trials about 200 miles off the coast of Cape Cod, Mass.

Former Nutley police officer Steve Rogers was in the U.S. Naval Reserves for 23 years and attained the rank of lieutenant commander in the Office of Naval Intelligence.

Ira W. Rubel, an American printer, quite by accident discovered a new way to print better than the conventional methods.

Raphael Rudd, a Nutley native, with multiple albums to his credit, was a classically trained international pianist and harpist whose talent led him to collaborate and earn respect of musicians around the world.

Nelson W. Rummel landed Normandy beach on D-Day, June 6, 1944. The war took him through France, Luxembourg, Belgium, Germany, and Czechoslovakia.

Most Reverend Michael A. Saltarelli, DD, Bishop of Wilmington, Del., served at Holy Family Church in Nutley from June 1960 to August 1977.

Richard R. Sarles, former Executive Director of NJ Transit is a 1963 graduate of Nutley High School. Sarles was appointed GM and CEO by the Washington Metropolitan Area Transit Authority in January 2011.

"Uncle Fred" Sayles lived on Satterthwaite Avenue in Nutley, and is probably best known for narrating the silent Farmer Gray cartoons on

Junior Frolics on Channel 13.

Nutley born Joseph Luke Scarpa of Spatz Avenue was a professional wrestler whose career started in 1947 when he joined the National Wrestling Alliance under the ring name "Joltin' Joe Scarpa."

Peter C. Scarpelli began public service as a commissioner in 1983. In 2000, he was elected as the 14th Nutley mayor. In 2004, he was re-elected to his seventh consecutive term and completed 25 years in office

Ralph Scognamillo has been in business in Nutley for nearly 30 years. In 2006, he moved J & R Towne Auto to Centre Street and Union Avenue, forgoing gas sales to concentrate on auto repairs.

Dr. Ronald J. Scrudato has been the director of New York University's Environmental Research Center at Oswego, New York since 1977.

Captain Abraham Speer sold a 27-acre portion of his 80-acre estate, which included the house, to John M. Vreeland. The house is known as the Vreeland Homestead, or former Womens Club on Chestnut Street.

Linda Stamato is the co-director of the Center for Negotiation and Conflict Resolution at the Edward J. Bloustein School of Planning and Public Policy at Rutgers University.

Capt. George J. Stanford served as athletic director of Nutley High school for 23 years. Football was his favorite sport and under his guidance Maroon teams made outstanding records in the metropolitan area.

Ed Stecewicz loved Nutley. In more than 10 years as an active Nutley Historical Society member, he served as president and museum director.

Martha Kostyra Stewart grew up on Elm Place, a short walk across the railroad tracks to the frozen Mud Hole where locals skated on cold winter evenings. She is the publisher of Martha Stewart Living magazine.

Frank R. Stockton became a best-selling author of novels and short stories. He lived at 203 Walnut Street, where he wrote his most famous piece "The Lady, or the Tiger?"

Eaton Stone, one of the best known circus men in the country died Aug. 6, 1903, at his home on Kingsland Road which became the site of Hoffman La-Roche.

Alix Strachey, née Sargant-Florence, with her husband translated into English of the works of Sigmund Freud. She was born in Nutley, to musician Henry Smyth Florence and painter Mary Sargant Florence.

Life-long Nutley resident Jean Thomas adopts retired racing greyhounds.

Ann Troy was one of the founders of the Nutley Historical Society in 1945, and was an essential part in creating a museum in which to collect and preserve genetic information, historical objects, and private papers, etc.

In 1912, Laura Tuers leased the Vreeland homestead to the Womens Club for meetings and social events.

Singer Frankie Valli and his family lived on Friedland Road in Nutley in the 1960s. Born Francesco Stephen Castelluccio in Newark, N. J., he grew up in a public housing project -- Stephen Crane Village.

Bastien van Giesen was the first to live in The Vreeland House more than 250 years ago. Built of locally quarried brownstone, the home was originally thought to have been constructed by Jacob Vreeland.

Juriaen Thomasse Van Riper received a grant patent on March 16, 1684, for land extending from the Third River up the Passaic to the Falls.

Geerat J. Vermeij is one of the world's preeminent scientists in ecology, malacology and biology. He taught at the University of Maryland, beginning as an instructor and advancing to Professor of Zoology.

Dr. Lynne Viola, a specialist in 20th century Russian history who speaks Russian fluently, is a 1973 graduate of Nutley High School. Her research interests include women, peasants, political culture and Stalinist terror.

Jacob Vreeland was the first Vreeland to settle in this area and the man who built Bend View, the Vreeland estate on the banks of the Passaic River.

John M. Vreeland bought a 27 acre portion of land from Capt. Abraham Speer, who was not only his brother-in-law but under whom he had served as a private in his company during the Revolution.

Warren Vreeland, the last direct male in the Nutley line, died in the Vreeland Homestead home in 1909. In 1912, his daughter Laura Tuers leased the property to the Womens Club for meetings and social events.

John Walker was a beloved educator in Nutley who displayed love and concern for every child. He died in May 2000. The Franklin Middle School was renamed the John H. Walker Middle School in his honor.

Al C. Welenofsky, a resident of Nutley since 1940, a graduate of Nutley High School, is an adventurer, mountaineer and canoeist, who has canoed more than 11,027 miles.

Journalist Phil White covered Nutley news for nearly five decades ultimately creating his own hyper-local news outlet NJHometown while assisting community organizations receive more attention.

Weary Willie was a member of a 19th Century traveling circus that visited town every year. According to folk lore, Weary Willie was a sad-sack clown who walked around with a bag of gold coins. If anyone could make him smile, they would get all the gold coins in his bag.

CBS TV anchor Chris Wragge spent a lot of time here on Whitford Avenue and played all junior football and farm and little league baseball in town.

BIBLIOGRAPHY

BOOKS

Brown, Elizabeth Stow. *The History Of Nutley*, Nutley Board of Education, 1907
Buccino, Anthony and Buccino, Andrea. *Nutley Sons Honor Roll-Remembering the Men Who Paid For Our Freedom*, Cherry Blossom Press, 2004, 2009.

Canfora, Nicole T. *Images of America: Belleville*

Demmer, John. *Images of America-Nutley*

Gabriele, Michael. *The History of the Nutley Velodrome*,

Peters, Marilyn, and O'Connor, Richard, *Then and Now Nutley*,

Troy, Ann. *Nutley Yesterday-Today*, Nutley Historical Society, Nutley, New Jersey, 1961

NEWSPAPERS
Newark Evening News
The New York Times
The Nutley Journal
The Nutley Sun
Star-Ledger

ONLINE SOURCES
Internet Movie Data Based, IMBD.com
NJ.com
NorthJersey.com
Wikipedia, the free encyclopedia

ABOUT THE AUTHOR

Nutley, NJ, author Anthony Buccino's stories of the 1960s, transit coverage and other writings earned four Society of Professional Journalists Excellence in Journalism awards. He published five essay collections, three book length photo collections, three military history books and seven full-length poetry collections.

The writer, editor, photographer, historian, wordsmith writes with clarity and humor in his columns and verse about growing up in the second half of the 20th Century. His photography earned him the nickname "New Jersey's 'Anvil Adams'."

Born in Belleville, the Nutley resident spent 12 years editing business news copy at Dow Jones & Co. and *The Wall Street Journal* professional web pages. He worked for several years as an associate editor at TheStreet.com. He has written in online publications about life and growing up in northern NJ. For five years he wrote about commuting and transit in metro New York-New Jersey.

His Nutley books include:

NUTLEY SNAPSHOTS In Plain View, Volume One

Nutley Notables - The men and women who made a memorable impact on our hometown, Nutley, New Jersey — Volume One

Nutley Sons Honor Roll - Remembering the Men Who Paid for Our Freedom

Belleville and Nutley in the Civil War

Yountakah Country - A Poetic View of Nutley, Old and New

Made in the USA
Middletown, DE
11 January 2019